6-49

KU-198-095

The Racism Issue

1/11/01

ISSUES

(formerly Issues for the Nineties)

Volume 6

Editor

Craig Donnellan

Independence

Educational Publishers

Cambridge

3013050503923740

OR X
10/10/

300155
SHL

First published by Independence
PO Box 295
Cambridge CB1 3XP
England

© Craig Donnellan 2001

Copyright
This book is sold subject to the condition that it shall not,
by way of trade or otherwise, be lent, resold, hired out or otherwise
circulated in any form of binding or cover other than that in which it
is published without the publisher's prior consent.

Photocopy licence
The material in this book is protected by copyright. However, the
purchaser is free to make multiple copies of particular articles for instructional
purposes for immediate use within the purchasing institution.
Making copies of the entire book is not permitted.

British Library Cataloguing in Publication Data
The Racism Issue – (Issues Series)
I. Donnellan, Craig II. Series
305.8'00941

ISBN 1 86168 165 8

Printed in Great Britain
The Burlington Press
Cambridge

Typeset by
Claire Boyd

Cover
The illustration on the front cover is by
Pumpkin House.

CONTENTS

Introduction

The Racism Issue is the sixth volume in the **Issues** series. The aim of this series is to offer up-to-date information about important issues in our world.

The Racism Issue looks at the issue of racism in the community and in the workplace. The book also covers ways to tackle racism.

The information comes from a wide variety of sources and includes:
Government reports and statistics
Newspaper reports and features
Magazine articles and surveys
Literature from lobby groups
and charitable organisations.

It is hoped that, as you read about the many aspects of the issues explored in this book, you will critically evaluate the information presented. It is important that you decide whether you are being presented with facts or opinions. Does the writer give a biased or an unbiased report? If an opinion is being expressed, do you agree with the writer?

The Racism Issue offers a useful starting-point for those who need convenient access to information about the many issues involved. However, it is only a starting-point. At the back of the book is a list of organisations which you may want to contact for further information.

*****

Discrimination and prejudice

Information from the British Humanist Association

We all evolved together

Humanists, like the vast majority of people, accept the scientific theory of evolution. They believe that human beings are more alike than they are different from each other – we are all members of the same species, *Homo sapiens* (which means 'wise man'!), and we are all descended from the same ancestors, so, in effect, we are all distantly related to each other. We also evolved as a gregarious species, which means that we live in large groups and have to work with each other.

Prejudice

Prejudice, which amounts to judging people or groups without reason or knowledge, and which leads to discrimination, must be wrong. It would be inaccurate to say that people are equal, when we are all so obviously different: some people are tall, others short; some people can run very fast; some are good at passing exams; some are male, others are female; some are black, others white – and so on. But reasonable people believe that all people should be judged as individuals, and treated with equal consideration and given equal opportunities in life.

What exactly is discrimination?

Discrimination is not in itself a bad thing. It means something like 'careful judgement and choice, noticing differences'. For example, if you are buying a present for a friend, it's a good idea to be a bit discriminating, to look carefully and choose something that you think s/he'd really like, not just the first thing you see.

Discrimination becomes unfair when we make a big deal out of irrelevant differences between people so that it affects their education or employment or housing or status in society. If, for example, we decide that we aren't going to employ women to do certain jobs just because they're women, or that only people belonging to certain races can live in this country or on some housing estates, or that homosexuals can't join the army, that is unfair discrimination. Humanists believe in judging individual situations, not in stereotyping and discriminating against entire groups of people.

Occasionally people may have reasons for discrimination. For example, a woman might be the most suitable person for the job of counsellor at a women's refuge. The law permits this kind of sensible discrimination.

'Political correctness'

(Or 'PC', as it is sometimes called) has been criticised a great deal. Political correctness means using words or behaving in such a way as to avoid giving offence – as such it is just good manners. Some words are offensive and hurtful, and encourage prejudice and discrimination. PC can become objectionable if it is a substitute for action to remedy a problem, or if it becomes an excuse for unfair discrimination.

Some 'isms'

Some forms of unfair discrimination are given the suffix 'ism': racism, sexism, ageism. Some people who support animal rights use the word 'speciesism' to describe how we discriminate unfairly against other species. Not all forms of prejudice or discrimination have convenient labels, though: people can also be discriminated against because of their faith or religion (or lack of faith and religion) or political beliefs, physical disabilities, or their social origins (snobbery is a form of unfair discrimination).

Why do prejudice and discrimination exist?

Human beings like to feel part of a group, and sometimes, in order to achieve this, put up barriers to protect

the group identity and keep out outsiders. All groups, tribes and nations tend to do it, and religious communities do not have a very good record on this: they have discriminated against women and homosexuals, or people of different religions or races, and invented discriminatory caste systems. Human beings also tend to fear, or at least feel cautious towards, anything or anyone very new or different. This may be natural, but that doesn't mean it's good or that human beings can't progress beyond these rather primitive emotions.

Co-operation, not conflict

Human beings need to co-operate and to give every individual the chance to flourish and play their part

If we treated people of all beliefs and races and ages with respect, the world would be a more peaceful place

in society, if we are all to be happy and prosper. Humanists promote happiness and fulfilment in this life because they believe it's the only one we have. Humanists believe in using reason and compassion to solve problems. It is in everyone's interest to oppose prejudice and discrimination, not just those on the receiving end of it. If we treated people of all beliefs and races and ages with

respect, the world would be a more peaceful place.

Education can reduce the ignorance and fear that cause unfair discrimination and prejudice. We are fortunate now to have media which can inform us about people and events all over the world – different people need not seem strange or frightening in the way they might have to our great-grandparents. If you look around you with an open mind, you will see that life is much more interesting because we are not all identical.

• The above information is from the British Humanist Association. See page 41 for their address details.
© British Humanist Association (BHA)

Racism today

Information from Show Racism the Red Card

In today's society racism takes many forms. There's the brutal, vicious side that leads to racist attacks and murders like that of Stephen Lawrence.

There's the blatant everyday racism directed at people in the form of name calling, abuse and harassment.

Then the sometimes more subtle racism that exists in many of our institutions, what has come to be known as institutional racism.

All forms of racism involve making assumptions and generalisations (stereotypes) about people who are a different colour. These stereotypes are often used to justify excluding people from opportunities, resources and power. This often leads to black and Asian people being deprived of decent housing, education and jobs.

Racist attacks

It is estimated that there are over 130,000 racially motivated crimes a year in the UK. Racial abuse and threatening behaviour can occur in a variety of locations including: places of study and work; in or near home; places of entertainment, on public transport or on the street.

Recent victims of racist murders include Michael Menson, a talented black musician who was set alight by racists, and Ricky Reel who was drowned. In both cases their families have had to fight long and hard to have these deaths recognised as racially motivated murders.

Perhaps the most well-known recent case of a racist murder is that of Stephen Lawrence. In April 1993, Stephen, a black 17-year-old student, was waiting at a bus stop with a friend in Eltham, south-east London. They were attacked by a gang of five white youths shouting racist abuse. Although his friend, Duwayne Brooks, escaped, Stephen was stabbed to death by the racists.

There has now been a lot of publicity about the case but

Stephen's killers have still not been brought to justice. Neville and Doreen Lawrence, Stephen's parents, despite facing lots of obstacles – including the police, the courts and the legal system – have struggled for justice for their son.

While justice can never be done until those who murdered Stephen have been punished for their crime, his case, the sheer determination of his parents and the public inquiry into his murder, have brought the issue of racism onto the national agenda in a way not seen in decades.

Institutional racism

'The collective failure of an organisation to provide an appropriate and professional service to people because of their colour, culture or ethnic origin. It can be seen or detected in processes, attitudes and behaviour which amount to discrimination through unwitting prejudice, ignorance, thoughtlessness and racist stereotyping which disadvantage minority ethnic people' (Macpherson Report definition of institutional racism).

This is how the Stephen Lawrence Inquiry (also known as the Macpherson Report) has defined institutional racism. Published on 24 February 1999, the report details how many of the institutions in Britain, including the police, are riven with racism. Amongst the many recommendations made by the report to improve the situation are:

- That the police force take special measures to challenge racism and increase racial equality and police accountability.
- That all racist incidents should be reported, recorded and investigated, whether or not a crime has been committed.
- That the Crown Prosecution Service (CPS) should prosecute racist crimes.

- That education can play a key role in eradicating racism and the National Curriculum should better reflect the needs of a diverse society.
- That anti-racism strategies should be put in place in all schools.
- That local councils should use community initiatives to challenge racism.

Fact file:

- 25% of black people say they have been racially abused or threatened in the last 12 months.
- People of South Asian origin (e.g. people from Bangladesh, Pakistan and Sri Lanka) are 50 times more

likely than white people to be victims of racially motivated incidents.
- People of African and African-Caribbean origin are 36 times more likely to be victims of racially motivated incidents.
- 60 per cent of victims do not report racially motivated crime to the police.
- Black people are seven times more likely to be stopped and searched than whites.
- The above information is from a Video Resource Pack produced by Show Racism the Red Card. See page 41 for address details.

The rise of the Little Englanders

Xenophobic views are increasing, says survey, as figures reveal widening gap on nationality, race and foreign affairs

A sharp increase in the number of Little Englanders who do not identify themselves as British and tend towards racist and xenophobic views is disclosed today by the National Centre for Social Research in its annual survey of social attitudes.

As power devolved to Scotland and Wales over the first two years of Tony Blair's government, the proportion of English people saying they owed allegiance to England, not Britain, grew from 7% to 17%.

The researchers discovered no evidence of resentment in England about power passing to the Scottish parliament and Welsh assembly, but the figures suggested that 6m adults in England no longer subscribed to a British national identity.

More than a third of this group (37%) freely admitted to being racially prejudiced, compared with 17% of those who continued to assert their Britishness.

They were also much more likely to think that immigrants take jobs away from people who were born in Britain (70%), that it was 'bad' that

By John Carvel, Social Affairs Editor

people from ethnic minorities were getting ahead (26%), and that attempts to give equal opportunities

to blacks and Asians in Britain had 'gone too far' (46%).

The Little Englanders were also more likely to say it mattered a great deal to being English that people were white and born in England, with English parents.

Nearly three-quarters (73%)

THE REST OF YOU – FIND YOUR OWN PLANET!!

ENGLAND

wanted to keep the pound as Britain's only currency and 22% thought Britain should quit the EU altogether – a much more strongly Eurosceptic stance than among those acknowledging British nationhood.

The survey by John Curtice, of Strathclyde University, and Anthony Heath, of Oxford University, concluded: 'We have found that those who feel English are indeed different from those who feel British, being consistently more inclined to want to shut out the outside world. Indeed "Little Englanders" appear to be alive and well, if not yet very thick on the ground.'

By contrast 6% of those who described their ethnic origin as black and 7% of those who said they were Asian classified themselves as English, not British. More than a third said they were British, not English.

The survey found a quarter of people living in England thought Scotland should become completely independent, but the most common response to Scotland's status was indifference. More than half would be 'neither pleased nor sorry' if Scotland were to become completely independent.

'We have found that those who feel English are indeed different from those who feel British, being consistently more inclined to want to shut out the outside world'

A fifth of English people wanted independence for Wales, either inside or outside the EU. And a majority (54%) thought Northern Ireland's long-term interests would be with the rest of Ireland rather than as part of Britain.

But these reformist views did not lead to any great appetite for devolution within England, where 15% favoured regional assemblies and 18% wanted an English parliament.

'This is probably why the somewhat muted attempts by the Conservative party to identify itself as the party of English interests have met with an even more muted response,' the study said.

One reason why English nationalism might struggle to assert itself was a lack of potent symbols belonging exclusively to England after centuries of intertwined British culture.

More than half thought fox hunting and Guy Fawkes' night were English rather than British institutions. Paradoxically, a third thought the same about the Houses of Parliament, the centre of the British democratic state.

The survey, based on more than 3,000 interviews with a representative random sample of people in England, Scotland and Wales, was the 17th in the British social attitudes series.

A black and white issue

Anthony Appiah visits Newcastle and sees black and white united on the football kit but divided on the street

Many people have a negative view of Haringey. They see Tottenham as a 'ghetto' full of people from minority ethnic groups. We know parts of our borough are scruffy and run down but it's not all bad.

Haringey is an area where ethnic minorities can generally live in peace without suffering from too much torment and racism.

The problem is that many non-white people in Haringey feel they cannot move to other parts of the country.

They are afraid that if they migrate to a less mixed area they will face discrimination and rejection. My experiences prove that this is true.

My mother is white and my dad is black (from Ghana). My mother was raised in Leadgate, a predominantly white area not far from Newcastle. From the first time

---

By Anthony Appiah

I went there it was clear that many local people had a problem with the fact that I was mixed race. My mum was taunted and asked peculiar questions, even by her own friends. She felt that people looked on me as some sort of curiosity and this made her angry.

We had to go to Leadgate two or three times a year to visit my mum's family. So, as I grew older, I attempted to make friends there. To begin with I was shunned. It seemed that the other kids didn't want to be seen with someone who had darker skin than them.

Eventually I got to know a boy called Ian who lived next door to my grandma. We both liked wrestling and we were both loyal supporters of Newcastle United so we had a few things in common, which helped.

Ian showed me his favourite hangouts and we got to know each other quite well. When I asked him if I could meet some of his friends, he was somewhat reluctant to take me. When I eventually did meet them they were pretty friendly but there was one boy who continually gave me dirty looks and uttered things under his breath. To begin with I didn't do anything and just ignored it and we continued to meet and play football everyday.

One day, after a competitive tackle, this boy remarked, 'What are you doing, Blackie?' I couldn't ignore him any more.

I walked towards him shouting, 'Who are you calling that?' We got into an argument and this eventually led to a fight, which I won easily.

Not surprisingly for a coward who had just lost a fight, he ran home and called his mother. She came out and started shouting at me. When I finally got a word in edgeways I explained what had happened and told her that her son had used a racist insult. Instead of reprimanding her son, she replied, 'so what, you black b*****d?'

My mother then came out, fists raised and looking for a fight. The other woman immediately fled and my mum took me inside.

This is a perfect example of the way most racists behave. They are just ignorant cowards. If they are in a gang they will insult you and belittle you but when the tables are turned, they run off like weasels. Fighting is

not the best way to deal with racism but when you are faced with that sort of provocation, it can be very hard to control your temper.

If someone is being racist towards you the best way to deal with the situation is to tell a teacher or parent or, if this racism leads to violence, tell the police.

I have never been the victim of racism in Haringey. At my school,

D&K, if you're racist, whether white on black or black on white, other people end up picking on you!

So, next time you hear people from outside Haringey calling our area a ghetto, remember to tell them that at least there aren't as many ignorant racists here as there are in other parts of the country.

© *Exposure Magazine*

Nazi piece of work

Patrick Nono writes about racism

Q. *What have Stephen Lawrence, Martin Luther King and Adolf Hitler got in common?*

A. Racism. Hitler was a racist leader, Stephen Lawrence was a victim of racism and Martin Luther King was a man dedicated to fighting racism.

So what exactly is racism? Well, in the dictionary racism is defined as hostile and oppressive behaviour towards people because they belong to a different race. In simple words it means people hating each other because they are different.

Racism is common in many places around the world. In America up until the time of Martin Luther King and his Civil Rights movement racial segregation was legal. If you were a black person you weren't allowed to eat in most restaurants or

sit in certain seats on the bus. This is something we can't imagine happening these days.

Although discrimination in this country may have decreased it still happens and when it does it's very shocking to the people who experience it. An example of the serious-

---

Racism is defined as hostile and oppressive behaviour towards people because they belong to a different race. In simple words it means people hating each other because they are different

---

ness of this form of hatred occurred recently when someone planted nail bombs in three places around London where there is a high concentration of minority groups. You may have heard about this but here's a quick recap.

The first place bombed was Brixton where the bomber is believed to have targeted the large black community there. The second bomb was in Brick Lane, Hackney, next to Haringey. This was targeted against the large Asian and Jewish communities. The third bomb was in London's Soho and was aimed at gay people. Four people were killed in the Soho attack and none of them were black, Asian, Jewish or gay!

Maybe these idiots should learn that bombs can't tell a person's colour or sexual preference. They just go off – and kill whoever's in the way.

The people responsible for this outrage are called 'Neo-Nazis'. 'Neo' means new and, if you remember your history lessons, you'll know that the 'Nazis' were a German political party that came to power during 1933 lead by Mr Hitler. These Nazis were responsible for the extermination of millions of Jews, gays and gypsies during the Second World War, in gas chambers, prisons and concentration camps.

The London bombings were taken very seriously by Londoners. And one good thing to come out of the tragedy is the coming together of many different people from many different backgrounds.

Londoners knew that they had to put their differences aside, put their heads together and fight a common evil – an evil that had to be stopped!

Although the police aren't everyone's best friend, people were happy to see them working so hard to investigate and arrest suspects as fast as they could.

You might think that it's only white people who are capable of discrimination. This is not true. People from ethnic minorities are also guilty of this, in different ways. For example, many people from ethnic minorities have homophobic beliefs (they hate gay people).

Nowadays you can find racist material in a lot of places, particularly the internet where neo-nazis encourage people to be racist. While I was doing some research for this article I tried to enter a racist site and a sign appeared saying, 'Whites only'. I'm black but I took no notice. It was a crap site anyway, our Michael (webmaster) could create much better!

I was shocked by what I saw. This offensive material can be accessed by anyone in their homes if they've got a PC, a phone line and a modem. I know that racism isn't just going to stop but that doesn't mean we should stop trying. As a wise man once said: 'If at first you don't succeed try, try, try again.'

I leave you with a question. What would have happened if Martin Luther King had been assassinated before he said the famous words: 'I have a dream'?

One thing I know is that Ian Wright wouldn't have been able to make a One2One TV advert. Think about it . . .

• The above information is from *Exposure Magazine* which can be accessed on the internet at www.exposure.org.uk

© *Exposure Magazine*

Race crime

Huge rise in race crime, reveals government

Racist incidents reported to the police rose by 107% last year, the Home Office disclosed today.

The total number of race crimes spiralled from 23,049 in 1998/99 to nearly 48,000 the following year in England and Wales, a new report shows.

In some police forces, the increases were huge – up 459% in West Mercia and 364% in Devon and Cornwall – and none of the 43 forces showed a reduction.

A separate report on how police are dealing with race and homophobic crime, and with recruiting ethnic minority staff, found most forces were doing well.

However, more effort was needed to end 'complacency regarding disproportionality in the use of stop-and-search tactics' and in retaining and promoting ethnic minority staff.

North Yorkshire was found to be failing in six of the 10 areas examined in the study and City of London police were failing in five.

Gwent Police were failing in eight areas, but were rated good in two and satisfactory in one.

Meanwhile, the race statistics showed more than 818,000 stop-and-searches were recorded by police, down from more than 1m the previous year.

In some police forces, the increases were huge – up 459% in West Mercia and 364% in Devon and Cornwall – and none of the 43 forces showed a reduction

---

Police use of stop-and-search tactics – criticised in the Macpherson report into the racist murder of black teenager Stephen Lawrence for targeting ethnic minorities more frequently than whites – fell by 40% in the Metropolitan police area and

14% in the rest of England and Wales.

Black people were five times more likely to be stopped and searched than whites and four times more likely to be arrested.

Nearly 60% of the people arrested by the Met for robbery were black, said the report.

Home secretary Jack Straw said that the figures 'reflected the different breakdown of who is committing robbery on the streets of London'.

Figures show black people accounted for 57.2% of arrests for robbery in the Met's area compared to an average of 28.2% in the whole of England and Wales.

'In London, there's bound to be a higher proportion of black people stopped for street crime because a higher proportion of black people commit street crime – that is not because they are black but because of their social background, age group and educational attainment,' said Mr Straw.

Commenting on the large rise in recorded race incidents, Home Office statistician Professor Paul

Wiles said: 'This increase most probably reflects better reporting and recording of incidents rather than an absolute increase in the numbers.

'The new simplified definition a racist incident – any incident is racist if perceived to be so by the victim or any other person – may have assisted officers in better identifying such incidents.'

Evidence from the British Crime Survey indicated that racist incidents were falling, he added. Mr Straw said that the sharp rise in the reporting of racial incidents was 'good news' because it showed an increasing confidence on the part of minorities that their concerns would be dealt with by the police.

He told BBC Radio 4's *World at One*: 'We know from the British Crime Survey that the total amount of racial crime seems to have gone down a bit.

'Why has the recording doubled? Because it shows an increased confidence by the black and Asian population to report these incidents and then have something done about them.'

He dismissed as 'utter nonsense' suggestions that the recent rise in violent offences was directly linked to a drop in the use of stop-and-search by police wary of being branded racist in the wake of the Macpherson Report.

Claims that police were being required to conform to the strictures of 'political correctness' were a 'smokescreen' put up by right-wingers who wanted to allege that the police had 'gone soft on the black community', but did not have the guts to say so openly, he said.

He added: 'Robbery has gone up in areas where there are no black people at all.

'It happens that the police division with the highest rate per thousand for robberies is Newcastle upon Tyne Central, where there are virtually no black people.

'There is a problem with robbery and it has got to be dealt with, and where the people committing the robberies happen to be black, the police have got to be able to deal with that as effectively and forcefully as if these people were white.'

Stopping and searching of people about whom police had a reasonable suspicion was backed both by the Home Office and by the Macpherson Report, said Mr Straw.

The real change in the use of stop-and-search since Macpherson was that it was being targeted more accurately than before, he said.

'Although the numbers have come down, the arrest rate has gone up, and that's good news,' said Mr Straw.

'For example, in respect of black people in London, (the police) success rate has improved by a quarter. In the previous year, just 13% of those stopped and searched were then arrested. That has now gone up to 17%.'

Mr Straw conceded that improvements in police recruitment of ethnic minorities 'could be faster', but said he remained confident the targets for recruitment would be met.

© *Guardian Newspapers Limited 2001*

Racial crime vs. ethnic population

The table below shows the number of racist incidents in England and Wales according to the size of the ethnic minority population

Constabulary	Size of ethnic population	Per cent affected by racist incidents
1) Northumbria	14,700	7.88
2) South Wales	24,900	6.43
3) Devon and Cornwall	8,900	6.04
4) Cheshire	8,600	4.90
5) Durham	3,900	4.56
6) Cumbria	2,000	4.25
7) Merseyside	19,900	4.13
8) Norfolk	6,400	3.95
9) Sussex	25,300	3.69
10) Avon and Somerset	25,200	3.52
11) Dyfed Powys	2,900	3.41
12) Dorset	5,800	3.19
13) West Mercia	14,800	3.14
14) Northamptonshire	19,100	3.13
15) Kent	30,300	3.02
16) Gwent	7,400	2.88
17) Gloucestershire	9,100	2.84
18) Humberside	7,900	2.72
19) Hampshire	24,500	2.67
20) Wiltshire	9,200	2.40
21) Nottinghamshire	29,900	2.39
22) Cambridgeshire	22,800	2.28
23) Hertfordshire	31,000	2.27
24) Cleveland	9,400	2.17
25) North Yorkshire	4,800	2.00
26) Met*	1,189,300	1.97
27) North Wales	4,200	1.90
28) Essex	23,000	1.87
29) Suffolk	13,100	1.79
30) South Yorkshire	31,100	1.79
31) Greater Manchester	135,500	1.72
32) Lancashire	55,400	1.65
33) Surrey	21,200	1.59
34) Derbyshire	24,300	1.58
35) West Yorkshire	145,300	1.46
36) Leicestershire	69,800	1.26
37) Thames Valley	85,200	1.17
38) Staffordshire	17,400	1.16
39) Warwickshire	15,300	0.98
40) Bedfordshire	41,200	0.73
41) West Midlands	287,200	0.54
42) Lincolnshire	4,400	0.43

* Includes figures for City of London Police

Source: *Statistics on Race and the Criminal Justice System, Home Office*

Race and the criminal justice system

Annual statistics for 2000 published by the Home Office

Statistics giving the most comprehensive picture to date of how people from minority ethnic backgrounds fare under the criminal justice system are published by the Home Office today.

Statistics on Race and the Criminal Justice System provides a breakdown by ethnicity (and by police force) of stops and searches, victims and homicide, arrests and cautions, prosecutions and sentencing, prison population, racist incidents and crimes, police complaints and practitioners in the criminal justice system.

This year's publication sees the inclusion of new data relating to arrests figures, Crown Prosecution Service decisions on young defendants, ethnic monitoring of magistrates' courts' decisions, information on the religious affiliation of prisoners, ethnicity of those on home detention curfew or on parole, first full year of figures for racially aggravated offences, racist incidents in prison, and deaths in police custody.

Key findings for 1999/2000 include:

- 800,000 stops and searches were recorded by the police, of which 8 per cent were of black people, 4 per cent Asian, and one per cent 'other' non-white origin. Black people were five times more likely to be stopped and searched by the police than white people;
- Most police forces showed an overall increase in the proportion of stops and searches which led to an arrest. Compared with 1998/99 the number of stops and searches in the Metropolitan Police area fell by 41 per cent for white people and Asians and by 35 per cent for black people. In the rest of England and Wales the falls were less with an average

fall of about 14 per cent for white people and Asians and 10 per cent for black people.

- Over the last three years police have provisionally recorded 2,003 homicides, of which 10 per cent were of black people, six per cent Asian and three per cent 'other' non-white ethnic origin. 15 homicides were recorded as being racially motivated over this period;

Ethnic minorities are under-represented in all grades as employees in the police service, prison service and in senior posts in all the criminal justice agencies

---

- 1.3 million arrests for notifiable offences took place, of which seven per cent were of black people, four per cent Asian and one per cent 'other' non-white origin. Black people were four times more likely to be arrested than white or other ethnic groups. Eight per cent of arrests for notifiable offences resulted from a stop and search under the Police and Criminal Evidence Act;
- Police cautioned about 180,000

people for notifiable offences of which six per cent were black people, four per cent Asian and one per cent 'other' non-white ethnic origin;

- Data from five pilot areas on magistrate court decisions indicated that white defendants were more likely to be convicted (65 per cent) than black or Asian defendants (both 56 per cent);
- In June 1999, ethnic minorities accounted for 18 per cent of the male prison population and 25 per cent of the female prison population. Black and Asian prisoners tended to be younger than white prisoners. White and Asian prisoners tended to be serving shorter sentences than black prisoners;
- Racist incidents recorded by the police rose by 107 per cent to 47,810 in 1999/00. This is likely to reflect better reporting and recording of such incidents;
- During the first full year of recording for the new racially aggravated offences 21,750 offences were recorded – one-half were offences of harassment which included public order offences of threatening or disorderly behaviour, of which one-third were detected;
- Nine per cent of complaints against the police in 1999/00 were from black people, six per cent from Asian and two per cent from other ethnic minority groups; and
- Ethnic minorities are under-represented in all grades as employees in the police service, prison service and in senior posts in all the criminal justice agencies. However the proportion of ethnic minorities in criminal justice agencies has continued to improve over previous years.

© Home Office

Police 'show no race bias in searches'

By John Steele, Crime Correspondent

Police are not generally biased against ethnic minorities when they stop and search people, new Government research shows.

A white person is more likely to be stopped, according to extensive Home Office studies. This undermines a central assertion by Sir William Macpherson, who led the Stephen Lawrence murder inquiry, that 'discrimination is a major element in the stop and search problem'.

Ethnic minorities, particularly black men, have always been stopped and searched in higher proportion to their share of the overall population and this has led to accusations of discrimination. But the study says that this is a misleading statistic. The essential point is the 'availability' of people on the streets to be searched, usually at night, it says.

Researchers, using cameras trained on passers-by and traffic, supplemented by interviews, looked at the people on the streets and in cars in Greenwich and Hounslow in London, Leicester, Ipswich and in the Chapeltown area of Leeds.

The available population was shown to be 'very different' from the resident population, with more young people and, significantly, higher numbers of people from ethnic minorities. Judged on resident, census-based populations, all five areas showed disproportionately high stopping and searching of black people and mostly lower targeting of white people.

But, based on the measure of available population, the picture was reversed. This led the report to say that the findings 'did not suggest any general pattern of bias against those from minority ethnic backgrounds. This was true for minority ethnic backgrounds as a whole, as well as particular groups.

'Asian people tended to be under-represented in those stopped or searched, compared to their numbers in the available population, with some notable exceptions.' The picture for black people was 'mixed'.

> **The findings 'did not suggest any general pattern of bias against those from minority ethnic backgrounds. This was true for minority ethnic backgrounds as a whole, as well as particular groups'**

In Greenwich and Chapeltown they were mostly under-represented, but in Hounslow and Ipswich they were stopped in vehicles at a higher rate than their available numbers would suggest.

The report says: 'Perhaps surprisingly, the most consistent finding across sites was that white people tended to be stopped and searched at a higher rate than their numbers in the available population would predict.'

The research highlights instances of unfairness and bias, as well as inept and rude or aggressive conduct by officers, which caused friction with ethnic minorities. But, overall, it finds that there is no 'general pattern of bias' – a view that will be welcomed by police officers who believe that the debate does not recognise the reality of policing inner-city streets.

Police tend to use stop and search 'more or less appropriately' in areas of high crime, which are often areas with high ethnic minority populations, the report says. The overall research runs to hundreds of pages in six reports.

Joel Miller, the author of the fifth report, *Profiling Populations Available for Stops and Searches*, stresses that it does not dismiss the possibility of discrimination in police practice. He says: 'One reaction to this research is that police forces do not have too much to worry about.

'However, in many respects, the findings are a problem for the police. Most significantly, they suggest that disproportionality is to some extent a product of structural factors beyond police control. Therefore, they may lack the power to eliminate it by changing their practices.'

The structural problem resulted because the high crime areas patrolled by police tended to have larger ethnic communities. Officers were also exposed to more ethnic minority people in the available populations of those areas. The research found that forces which relied heavily on stop and search had no better clear-up rates than those that used it less.

Asylum seekers

Facts vs. myths

The newspapers would have us believe that a 'flood' of 'bogus' asylum seekers, 'benefit scroungers who are abusing our hospitality' are 'swamping Britain'. This negative language about asylum seekers and immigrants results in their dehumanisation, which is turning into the ugliest of all prejudices: racism. Here are some of the most common media myths nailed with simple facts.

Myth #1: 'Britain receives more than its share of refugees'

In fact . . . Many other European countries receive more refugee claimants than the UK, which in 1999 had around 74,000 applications. The number of asylum applications per 1,000 people brings the UK down to 9th place in Europe. In 1999, Liechtenstein received the highest number of asylum seekers – 16.3 per 1,000 inhabitants, followed by Luxembourg (6.8), Switzerland (6.5), Belgium (3.5) and the Netherlands (2.5). The UK ratio for 1999 was 1.5 asylum seekers per 1,000 inhabitants and Germany's was 1.16 (source: United Nations High Commission for Refugees). The majority of the world's refugees come from – and remain in – countries of the South. The following countries have each been hosting over a quarter of a million uprooted people in 1998, when around 58,000 asylum seekers reached Britain. For example, Iran received 1.9 million refugees. Jordan received 1.4 million; Pakistan received 1.2 million refugees. Gaza Strip had 746,000, Yugoslavia (FR) had 550,000 refugees and the US had 491,000 applications for asylum in 1998, followed by Guinea (430,000), Sudan (365,000), Russian Federation (324,000) and Ethiopia (313,000) (source: US Committee on Refugees (USCR)). Britain receives less than 1% of the world refugee population.

Myth #2: 'Majority of asylum claims in the UK are bogus'

In fact . . . More than half (54%) of decisions in 1999 resulted in protection being granted. The real figure, once successful appeals are taken into account, will be even higher. Most asylum seekers are refused not because their cases are bogus, but because they travelled through other countries on their way to Britain or because of lack of information and good legal advice.

Myth #3: 'They come here to claim our generous benefits'

In fact . . . This is the most common allegation against asylum seekers and refugees. Apart from being false, this statement is utterly offensive and racist. The belief that people claim asylum in the UK so they can live on benefits 30% below those considered good enough for UK citizens is laughable. It implies that they do not deserve better because of who they are and where they are from, and that 'out' poverty is too good for them. Asylum seekers are entitled only to the equivalent of 70% of Income Support and even this will be in the form of humiliating vouchers. In addition, asylum seekers are not allowed to apply for work for the first six months after their arrival and if they are waiting for an appeal they are also prohibited from working.

Myth #4: 'Refugees who come to the UK using false documents are bogus'

In fact . . . For many refugees fleeing persecution or death, a false travel document is the only means of escape. Often governments refuse to issue passports to known political dissidents – or imprison them if they apply. The fact that asylum seekers use false travel documents tells us nothing about whether the person is a refugee or not. Because refugees often cannot obtain all necessary papers, article 31 of the Geneva Convention prohibits governments

WANTED – A PLACE TO CALL HOME

from penalising refugees who use false documents. Most governments, including the UK, require travellers to have visas, creating an enormous obstacle for refugees trying to escape persecution. The more barriers governments put up to stop people travelling to their territory, the more refugees are forced to use false documents and turn to smugglers to help them escape.

Myth #5: 'Gypsies are just economic migrants abusing the system'

In fact . . . Refugees are people who have been forced to flee their homes by human rights abuses and all deserve the chance to start a new life. To say that some are less deserving than others is to say that some human beings are of less value than others. Article 14, Universal Declaration of Human Rights, states: 'Everyone has the right to seek and to enjoy in other countries asylum from persecution.'

Myth # 6: 'Asylum seekers are a burden on the economy and taxpayer'

In fact . . . The Government's own report for 1998 shows that the cost of supporting asylum including legal aid, welfare benefits, housing, health and education was 0.5 billion pounds or 0.33p out of income tax per week. Statistics on the number of asylum seekers who are working and contributing to the economy are not available.

Myth # 7: 'Increased immigration leads to an increase in crime'

In fact . . . There is no established connection between immigration and crime. Asylum seekers are just people like anyone else – a few end up in jail, most are law-abiding. In fact, they are themselves victims of physical and verbal abuse and racist attacks. The real scandal is that thousands of asylum seekers are locked up every year in detention centres while their cases are decided – even though they have committed no crime.

Myth # 8: 'Asylum system is a shambles'

In fact . . . Asylum system is a shambles, but to blame asylum

seekers for that would be like blaming all those who are ill and injured for the problems of the NHS. The Government is now facing a backlog of more than 100,000 claims. It is spending additional money, time and resources to keep asylum seekers isolated, excluded and poor in order to score cheap political points with 'middle England'.

Myth # 9: ' Thousands of asylum seekers disappear after they are refused'

In fact . . . Thousands of refused asylum seekers are being deported and removed from the UK every year. In 1999 30,685 persons were removed and deported. Many of them were sent back into the hands of their persecutors.

• The above information is from the BLINK (Black Information Link) web site which can be found at www.blink.org.uk which is produced by the 1990 Trust. See page 41 for their address details.

© The 1990 Trust

Ethnic minorities grow to 1 in 10

By Alan Travis, Home Affairs Editor

Next year's census is expected to show that minority ethnic communities total more than 5m people, or 10% of Britain's population, Jack Straw said yesterday.

The home secretary's 'best guess' of the growth in the black and Asian communities came as he confirmed the introduction of a race equality law directed against 'institutional racism' across the public sector, including schools, hospitals and broadcasting organisations such as the BBC.

The last census in 1991 estimated that Britain's minority ethnic population accounted for 7% of the population, at about 3.5m. Mr Straw said that in London the proportion probably now stood at around 20%; in some boroughs, and in his constituency of Blackburn in Lancashire, it was more than 50%.

Publishing the second annual report on progress in tackling racism since publication of the Macpherson inquiry into the murder of Stephen Lawrence, the home secretary said that the new figures would underline the scale to which Britain was a multiracial society.

Mr Straw said the report on 70 recommendations put forward by Macpherson showed 'encouraging progress in key areas, but we cannot afford to be complacent'. He said that, after two years, the 'breadth and depth of the change' required had become clear, and much more needed to be done within the police and elsewhere to ensure the reforms would stand the test of time. He acknowledged that the big four police forces – London, Manchester, the West Midlands and West Yorkshire – were falling short.

A consultation paper on the equality law, which comes into effect from April, confirms that major central and local government bodies will have to ensure their workforce reflects their communities, and policies and practices do not indirectly discriminate. The commission for racial equality is to be given powers to secure court orders where needed.

© Guardian Newspapers Limited 2001

Race and the workplace

Black and Asian people obtain more degrees than whites. So why do so few get senior jobs?

By Mabel Msonthi

The recent, and much-discussed, report by the Runnymede Trust on the future of multi-ethnic Britain rightly asked why so few black or Asian workers make it into senior positions in the workplace. So when it emerged last week that only one black person had worked on the report, and in a junior position – Helen Francis, an administrative assistant, who left the commission not long after the inquiry started – charges of hypocrisy were levelled. Robin Richardson, who edited the report, conceded: 'I am embarrassed. I agree with you that it doesn't look good.'

A response involving glass houses and stones is tantalisingly easy to trot out; investigating the central tenet of the report on equal opportunities in the workplace, however, is a modern-day Gordian Knot. With Ireland's 'anti-racist workplace week' coming up at the start of November, what is the real state of race equality in employment as we near the end of the first year of the new millennium?

'We have commissioned four reports over the last year which have revealed worryingly disproportionate levels of unemployment amongst black and Asian workers despite their degree level qualifications,' says a spokesperson for the TUC. Set against statistics gleaned from the Labour Force Survey commissioned by the Department for Education and Employment, which show that 21% of black and Asian people obtain degrees, compared with 16% of their white counterparts, the question of why they are still far less likely to make it to a senior role in the workplace is a pertinent one.

'The TUC set up a Rooting Out Racism hotline in June of this year and within five days we had received 450 calls, all recounting harrowing tales of workplace harassment and consistent examples of people being overlooked for promotion,' adds the spokesperson. 'There are many recommendations in the *Future of Multi-Ethnic Britain* report that need to be focused on by employers, not simply the one aspect [that of the contentious meanings of the word "British"] that was highlighted by most of the press.'

The commission's 417-page report contained recommendations aimed at ensuring that more black and Asian people are employed in senior roles. But how easy is it to enforce these policies? Alarmingly, it seems that the culture in many offices discriminates against people of ethnic minority origin often without companies and staff being aware of it.

According to the commission for racial equality, companies can discriminate indirectly by not advertising vacancies in certain areas of the press to attract applicants from a diverse background, thus ruling out a whole section of the population. Another example is word-of-mouth recruitment which often favours the well-connected and privileged in society – the very antithesis of equal opportunities for all. Similarly, enforcing rules which make all employees work on particular days of the year despite their religious beliefs can amount to indirect discrimination. So how should companies go about resolving anomalies in the recruitment process? Dianah Worman of the chartered institute of personnel & development emphasises the need for 'education and awareness-raising exercises in the workplace.

'Promoting race equality is all about valuing differences. It's in the interests of all businesses to communicate and deliver customer and client needs. Where are companies advertising? If this isn't pulling a diverse pool of applicants, where else could an organisation advertise?'

The economic aspect of this conundrum makes for fascinating reading. The *Business Benefits of Race Equality at Work* report is just one of those commissioned by the Department of Education and Employment for its Race Research for the Future series. It shows that an ethnically diverse workforce certainly pays: bottom-line savings of up to £250,000 were made by one of the companies interviewed. Companies selected for their efforts in increasing race equality demonstrated increased staff retention, reduced recruitment

shortages, improved employee relations, better customer service, increased sales and improved marketing.

While research tends to focus on senior positions, there is also concern about the state of equality within the support staff industry, particularly in the light of the Helen Francis incident. A study by the Institute for Employment Studies (IES), for example, looked into the effects of internal job advertising: in theory, it's fair, makes good use of available talent and shares opportunities around.

However, another report published in July reveals what really happens. As co-author Wendy Hirsh explains, 'Managers are used to choosing people and putting them where they want, based on who they know and what they know about them. Putting jobs on noticeboards and intranets won't stop managers bucking the system, especially if the system seems bureaucratic and slow.'

The IES has identified that what employees dislike most are managers who advertise a vacancy but have already really decided who they are going to appoint. This may mean strong candidates do not get looked at seriously. Particular members of the workforce may be more vulnerable to this discrimination as they possess fewer connections in the first place.

Listen to most support staff for any length of time and it soon becomes apparent that secretaries and administrators have a pretty hard time in terms of promotion prospects and increasing their areas of responsibility. The day-to-day experience of the average worker from an ethnic minority shows that these problems can be worse.

Elizabeth Johnson is black and has worked as a PA and team secretary for nearly nine years, in companies as diverse as a top public-sector union and a merchant bank. 'At the start of the recruitment process, I find that some consultancies want photographs to accompany your CV and it's at this point that my heart sinks. Too many times, I have nearly got the job but then a spurious reason for the vacancy no longer being available is given by

> *It is clear that discrimination by employers is one reason for ethnic minorities failing to get access to jobs and promotions*

the consultant, once the photos have been sent out.'

Once in a role, progression through the ranks is not always purely on merit. 'I seem to get along fine in team positions, but have found it harder to progress to senior roles such as a director's PA or an administrative manager,' says Johnson. 'I don't think I'm paranoid as nearly ten years of experience and a business administration degree from a red-brick university have still not enabled me to progress beyond team secretarial

roles. Meanwhile, many of my contemporaries are now office managers and senior executive PAs earning well in the region of £30k.'

Ultimately, there are no clear-cut solutions. One way to level out the playing field is to make sure someone with no axe to grind – a manager from another area or someone from personnel, say – acts as a quality control in the recruitment process to ensure fair play.

It is clear that discrimination by employers is one reason for ethnic minorities failing to get access to jobs and promotions despite often having the necessary qualifications. However, serious attempts to redress imbalances are now in place and with the economic benefits of equality self-evident, more and more organisations will find exclusion a high price to pay.

Harassment at work

Information from the Race Relations Employment Advisory Service (RREAS)

What is harassment?
Behaviour which is unwelcome or unacceptable and which results in the creation of a stressful or intimidating environment for the recipient.

What forms can harassment take?
- Verbal abuse
- Racist jokes
- Graffiti
- Embarrassing and/or insensitive comments
- Leering
- Physical contact
- Unwanted sexual advances
- Ridicule
- Isolation
- Victimisation

What should employers do?
Develop:
- A published, well-promoted policy statement with top management support
- Clear, fair and user friendly procedures for resolving problems quickly and confidentially
- Counselling, advice and support mechanisms for recipients
- Thorough and immediate investigation methods for all alleged incidents
- Swift, sensitive and effective remedies
- Appropriate grievance and disciplinary procedures
- A sustained programme of communication, monitoring and training.

Exposing racism at work

Information from the TUC

Introduction

Racism in the workplace is both widespread and serious; it affects the daily lives of too many people. This report, from the TUC's 'Root Out Racism' hotline, confirms what unions and their members have long believed. Black and Asian people are suffering personal pain and anguish, and are seeing their job prospects blighted by what the Macpherson Inquiry into Stephen Lawrence's murder called 'institutional racism'. Given the short time that the hotline was open (five days) it has only revealed the tip of an iceberg.

The hotline ran for five days in June and took nearly 450 calls. Callers reported how workplace racism had affected them on both a personal level and professionally. Many reported an appalling catalogue of verbal abuse. And some reported being the victims of actual physical violence. Callers said that racist abuse at work resulted in them taking time off sick with stress, depression and anxiety.

On a professional level callers complained about being refused references, not being informed properly about training, overtime or promotion opportunities and being unfairly monitored. If they complained some said they were deliberately isolated at work; ignored, victimised or even sacked. This report looks at who called the line and highlights some of the worst stories reported to the TUC. The report also looks at how the unions, employers and Government could tackle institutional racism.

The TUC set up its 'Stephen Lawrence Task Group', which ran the hotline, following the Macpherson Inquiry Report into Stephen Lawrence's murder. The Task Group's remit is to tackle institutional racism in the workplace, specifically dealing with recruitment, harassment, and promotion opportunities for black and Asian workers.

The Macpherson Inquiry report described institutional racism as: 'The collective failure of an organisation to provide an appropriate and professional service to people because of their colour, culture or ethnic origin which can be seen or detected in processes; attitudes and behaviour which amount to discrimination through unwitting prejudice, ignorance, thoughtlessness and racist stereotyping which disadvantages minority ethnic people.'

Case studies

Some of those who called the hotline were clearly distressed and seeking help, but the vast majority told stories that confirmed the Task Group's

---

Summary

- The TUC's Root out Racism hotline took 439 calls in five days. 55 per cent of callers were male and 45 per cent were non-union members.
- Just over half (53 per cent) the calls came from African/Afro-Caribbean workers. One in four calls came from Asian workers.
- Although not all callers gave details of the jobs they did, most callers came from professional (20 per cent) and clerical and secretarial (17 per cent) jobs. 14 per cent of callers worked in the personal and protective services (i.e. emergency services, security guards, catering workers and hairdressers).
- The majority of callers to the line (63 per cent) worked in the public sector. Almost one in ten callers (9 per cent) worked in transport and communications and another one in ten (9 per cent) worked in retail, hotels and catering.
- Calls came from all over the UK, although 62 per cent came from London. This fairly closely reflects the proportion of black and Asian people of working age in London (54 per cent).

---

view that racism in the workplace remains widespread. A number of callers used the facilities of the Urdu, Gujarati and Hindi interpreters. It took a great deal of courage for callers to ring up the hotline. And for many it was painful to recount their experiences, some broke down while speaking. Each caller was provided with a new advice leaflet entitled *Racism at work – a crime in anyone's language*: this leaflet is now available from the TUC's permanent Know Your Rights phone line.

Effects of racism at work

The effects fell into two categories. Firstly, personal, which included how people felt about themselves and its impact on their health. And secondly, its effects on their job prospects and futures.

Personal effects

Callers reported an appalling catalogue of:

- verbal abuse of race or religion; leaving racist literature around; taunting and name calling; mimicking accents and shouting
- being isolated, ostracised, sent to Coventry
- having food, tools, lockers etc. tampered with
- sickness often requiring long periods of sick leave including: stress, depression and anxiety
- actual physical violence, which in one case required time in hospital
- self-loathing, and feelings of self-destruction and inferiority.

Job prospects and future

Callers said that racism affected them both immediately and in the future and they reported:

- being refused references, sometimes after leaving a job resulting from undue pressure
- not being informed properly about training, overtime, or promotion opportunities; and procedures not being clear, or unfair, or arbitrary

- feeling unfairly monitored
- being denied or consistently overlooked for promotion; even though well qualified
- being downgraded without explanation
- feeling that they had to suffer in silence or risk being publicly isolated and refused a reference
- after making a complaint being labelled a 'trouble maker' or having 'a chip on their shoulder'.

Many of these callers were phoning with an unresolved problem, and sometimes they felt that they were not helped much either by management, unions, or advice agencies. However, some people reported a supportive response from other white workers to their plight, but this was sometimes seen as a sort of 'passive resistance'. In other words kind and supportive, but nothing being done, or effectively brushing the issue under the carpet. It seems that doctors have been helpful in recognising the effects on people's health and providing certificates for sick leave.

Hotline stories

Below are a selection of eight case studies drawn from calls to the hotline.

Financial service centre – London
A black female, finance service centre worker noticed that she was not receiving the right pay and that she had to prove herself and work much harder than all her white colleagues. She eventually worked her way into a management position where she was the only black female worker, but she was given staff that 'nobody else wanted'. She also found the office banter offensive. When speaking about going on holiday and lying on the beach one colleague said, 'Be careful that nobody picks you up and puts you into a black bag', and referred to 'turds on the beach'. This went along with a lot of 'very crude' talk from men about sex, women, masturbation etc. This kind of banter just continued and she became ill, very stressed and felt very isolated.

Engineering machinist – Merseyside
The only worker from an ethnic minority in his factory, a Chinese

man is called 'Mao', 'Chink', and 'Gook', and has had swarf put in his jacket pockets. He complained unsuccessfully to his section manager; the personnel department were not interested; and the directors have denied that this situation exists in the workplace. John is a shop steward and at one meeting, when there was a series of redundancies, he was told that one of the directors said this was the time to start ethnic cleansing. John has now been off work for several months with depression and has requested to work on night shift to get away from his tormentors.

Communications engineer – Manchester
The only black worker in his section faces racist comments every day at work. He's had 'nigger' written on his pigeonhole at work, but after complaining about it nothing was done for six months. The same was done to his locker. He complained about a notice scrawled in the toilets about joining the National Front, but his manager told him to clean it off himself. He says that people have urinated in his boots, there has been an attempt to set him alight, and he received death threats in post. One of the people responsible for sending these was caught and they admitted it to the police. He has been off work with stress and depression and felt suicidal, but has to think of his wife and kids.

Council worker – London
A black African man applied for promotion, he had all relevant

qualifications but was unsuccessful. He later found out that a white man with no qualifications was offered the job. He complained and was eventually given the job, but his boss asked him to bring in his passport to prove he was British. This followed the boss saying, 'I hate the black race coming in here to take our jobs.' He was upset because he was born in Britain, got his professional qualifications, and has lived here for 38 years. But he still suffers constant jibes and abuse at work, and it is just treated as a joke.

Occupational therapist – London
An Asian male occupational therapist has encountered indirect and direct forms of racism. For example a black girl was employed to work 37 hours weekly, but her hours were gradually cut down substantially, despite the fact that staff were needed. He was specifically told by his manager 'not to employ them' referring to blacks. He was told to carry out tasks which he was not required to do professionally, and when he complained he was verbally abused and accused of being 'aggressive'. His contract runs out soon and he has received a letter saying he will not be retained, due to 'allegations of misconduct'.

Clerical worker, holiday company – London
A black African woman was the only person from an ethnic minority with a long-term, temporary contract at a large holiday company, where one of her colleagues spoke within her earshot about joining the BNP. The

same colleague was constantly rude and abrupt when giving her tasks. Other colleagues later joined in with the verbal abuse, and began physically abusing and threatening her. Her manager ignored her complaints until she wrote to her local REC. As a result she was asked to leave for the sake of a happy workplace. Since then her agency has not given her long-term contracts, and she feels the incident has affected her job prospects.

Finance manager – London
An African man working as a finance manager received racist literature, telling him to leave, while still in his trial period. Later anonymous petitions were sent to higher managers demanding that black employees be removed from workforce. On the advice of his line manager he sent the literature to head office. They did nothing. He went to the police who said they too would investigate. But nothing was done about the problems.

Management consultant – London
An Asian male who works for a large management consultancy says that he was 'promoted to fail'. The firm had not one non-white, non-male partner, and only one non-white senior manager. He raised this issue and was told that the firm represented the make-up of the City. However he was promoted shortly before the company's statistics were submitted to the Equal Opportunities Council. He was subsequently moved sideways into an area where he had no experience, and was unable to deal with clients. He was fired soon afterwards, because the firm said it was moving into e-commerce, even though he has a degree in computer science. He believes that in order to keep the statistics right, ethnic minorities are promoted in the middle ranks before being moved sideways and out.

Tackling racism at work
Racial discrimination begins even before black and Asian people get a job, as racist recruitment procedures and attitudes provide an effective block to many to get a job at all. The TUC report *Black and excluded* revealed that racism is rife in the jobs market and has got worse during

the 1990s, despite growing employment opportunities. At 13 per cent, unemployment is two per cent higher among black and Asian workers than it was at the beginning of the 1990s. For their white counterparts unemployment has returned to its 1990 low point of six per cent. For some sections of the ethnic minority communities the situation is even worse – African-Caribbean men are 60 per cent unemployed in some inner-city areas.

In work black and Asian employees face not only direct racial harassment in the form of personal abuse, but also indirect discrimination, which means that they have considerably less chance of promotion. The TUC report *Qualifying for racism*, revealed that 21 per cent of black and Asian employees are educated to degree level, com-pared to just 16 per cent of their white counterparts. But despite receiving higher-level qualifications black and Asian employees face declining opportunities for career advancement. A growing 'management and supervisory gap' has grown during the 1990s between black and white workers.

The TUC's Stephen Lawrence Task Group is calling on employers and workplace representatives to recognise racism, to understand its effects, and to develop the confidence to deal with it. There are many lessons for all workplace stakeholders in seeking to achieve an ethnically diverse workforce that reflects the best in Britain's economy and society.

Policy implications and recommendations
Employers. It is in employers' interest to understand, acknowledge and challenge racism at work. Far from being simply 'politically correct', race equality at work means improved

services, increased productivity and profits. For example, as the results of the hotline show, the impact on those suffering racism can be devastating, inducing a bad working atmosphere and an unhealthy work environment resulting in lower productivity and poor services.

Employers that have a reputation for challenging racism will reap the benefits of increased efficiency, and increased sales, as demand for products may increase from ethnic minorities. And people will want to work for employers that reflect the diversity of British society. The cost of litigation and fines, in cases of direct and indirect racial discrimination, for employers can also be very high. Employers should:

Carry out voluntary ethnic monitoring to identify blockages in recruitment and promotion procedures; access to training and other workplace benefits; and to log complaints and outcomes in order to identify patterns of discrimination.

Introduce induction programmes elements that ensure that employees are fully aware and trained in understanding and resisting racism.

In the aftermath of the Stephen Lawrence Inquiry report, highlighting the impact of institutional racism in the Metropolitan Police, the Government introduced ethnic monitoring and targets into Government departments.

The Government should extend mandatory ethnic monitoring and targets to the private sector.

Unions
Trade unions have a key role in negotiating agreements with employers that challenge workplace racism. They must also represent black and Asian members effectively in cases of race discrimination: this will have the added benefit of encouraging potential members to join trade unions. Unions should ensure that all new officers, both elected and appointed, are fully trained in understanding racism and representing ethnic minority members.
• The above information is from the Trades Union Congress. See page 41 for their address details.

Racist firms keep black unemployment high

Ethnic minorities are not sharing in the new prosperity, despite growing labour shortages, as legislation fails to prevent employer discrimination

By Charlotte Denny

Black men are up to five times as likely to be unemployed as white men, according to government figures released today which suggest that ethnic minorities face widespread discrimination looking for jobs.

Eight years of steady economic growth have reduced the number of people out of work to just over 1m – a 20-year low. But while fewer than 6% of white men are unemployed, the figure for some groups of black men is as high as 27%, according to the office for national statistics.

Among women, the worst affected are those of Pakistani and Bangladeshi origin, nearly five times as likely as white women to be unemployed.

Labour market experts say these discrepancies show that equal opportunities legislation has failed to combat racism by employers.

Michael Oyeniyi lives in east London, a stone's throw from the City where the long economic boom has left firms short of skilled labour. But the 24-year-old personal computer technician has spent more than a year looking for work.

'Firms don't give me a chance to prove that I can do the job,' he said. 'At least 20% of it is being black. I know I can do the work.'

Mr Oyeniyi left his job as a Burger King manager and started looking for a job at the end of 1999 – when the government was proclaiming the healthy state of the labour market. With a computer qualification from Tower Hamlets College, completed part-time while at Burger King, he was confident he would find work.

During 12 months of determined hunting he has travelled as far as Gatwick for interviews but he has had no job offers, despite taking a further course which qualifies him as a Microsoft technician. He fixes computers for friends and neighbours, but what he really wants is to work in industry.

> *While fewer than 6% of white men are unemployed, the figure for some groups of black men is as high as 27%*

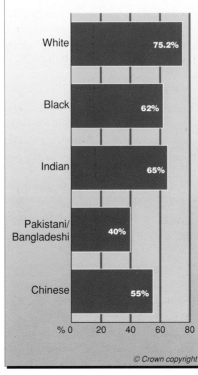

Employment

Employment rate (15-59/64) in Great Britain, 1998/99

White — 75.2%
Black — 62%
Indian — 65%
Pakistani/Bangladeshi — 40%
Chinese — 55%

% 0   20   40   60   80

© Crown copyright

The frustration of failing to get jobs for which he has all the requirements is showing. He wants companies to give him a chance. 'If I get to an interview, test me. I can do the work. If I don't pass that's OK.'

The problem which men such as Mr Oyeniyi face is often not lack of skills. Black men are likely to have higher qualifications than white men, according to government data.

David Blackaby, an expert on the labour market at the University of Swansea, says legislation designed to combat racial discrimination has failed. In the 30 years since the Race Relations Act was passed the position of black people in the labour market appears to have got worse.

'We assume in Britain that we don't discriminate and that there is a level playing field,' he said. 'But when you look at the numbers, it's quite frightening.'

Black people suffered disproportionately in the recession of the early 1990s. The unemployment rate for ethnic minority men soared to 25%, nearly two and a half times the rate for white men, and the gap between the two has remained steady since then, despite the recovery in the economy.

The recession hit black people harder, according to Dr Blackaby, because it gave firms the chance to discriminate. 'When there are lots of people out of work, it's easier for them to pick white workers over black or men over women.'

But Dr Blackaby is puzzled by why the gap between black and white workers has not closed as the labour market has improved. He thinks the government and firms are complacent about equal opportunities.

Firms are paying lip service to equal opportunities and diversity issues, according to a report published today by the Industrial Society. Employers say tackling racism and sexism is a priority yet fewer than half of the firms the society surveyed had a strategy for it.

'Our findings reveal that the rhetoric has yet to be translated into reality,' said Angela Ishmael, the report's author. 'Good intentions are simply not matched by sustained commitment in practice.'

The Trades Union Congress wants to see the provisions of the Race Relations Act toughened to make it harder for firms to favour white workers. 'These figures show that racism still blights the working lives of thousands of black and Asian people,' said John Monks, the TUC's secretary general.

But not everyone agrees that the problem is racism. Iftikhar Ahmed came to Britain from Pakistan eight

In the 30 years since the Race Relations Act was passed the position of black people in the labour market appears to have got worse

years ago and is looking for a job as a marketing manager. 'This country has less discrimination than many others,' he said. 'Usually it's too easy to blame others rather than looking at ourselves.'

Despite a master's degree in international business, Mr Ahmed's job hunt has been unsuccessful. But he remains convinced that with more IT skills, he will find work. 'If I don't update my qualifications, I shouldn't blame others or discrimination,' he said.

Jobless statistics

- The unemployment rate for white men was 6.9% of the workforce in spring 2000, while the rate for all ethnic minorities was 13%.

- Black men from countries other than Africa or the Caribbean have the highest unemployment rate at 26.6%. Bangladeshi men are next at 20.4%.

- Indian men have the lowest unemployment rate of any ethnic minority, at 7.2%.

- The unemployment rate for white women was 4.7%, while the rate for all ethnic minority women was 12.3%.

- Bangladeshi and Pakistani women have the highest rates of unemployment among ethnic minority women at 23.9%.

Racial discrimination

Information from the Industrial Society

Definition

Racial discrimination at work, under the Race Relations Act 1976, means discriminating on the grounds of race, colour, nationality or ethnic origin in terms of:
- recruitment and selection;
- terms and conditions of employment offered and provided;
- access to promotion, transfers and training;
- other benefits and services;
- dismissal; and
- subjecting the person to any other detriment.

Background

The Race Relations Act was introduced the year after the Sex Discrimination Act.
- The Commission on Racial Equality (CRE) was set up in 1976 to help deal with applications and complaints, and to assist employers in devising fair employment practices.
- Discrimination may be direct, when people are treated less favourably because of their race.

- It may also be indirect, when the conditions of employment make it difficult for members of certain racial groups to comply. The conditions may be fair in principle, but discriminatory in effect.
- Deliberate racial segregation is unlawful.
- Victimisation is also unlawful, for example when a person faces disciplinary action or dismissal as a result of bringing a complaint under the Act.
- The law applies to all employees, regardless of length of service or hours.

State of play

The Asylum and Immigration Act 1996 makes it a criminal offence for employers to knowingly employ people whose immigration status prevents them working in this country. This applies to those starting work since 27 January 1997.
- The employer can avoid prosecution by proving that before the employment began, the person produced one of the following to show their right to work: passport, travel document, birth certificate, residence or work permit, Home Office letter, document containing NI number, or other official letter.
- The TUC says that has already led to employers going beyond the Act's requirements and discriminating against those from ethnic minorities. It recommends employers should:
- not act as immigration officers and try to investigate the validity of a document;
- ask all employees to produce one of these documents and explain why; and
- treat all potential employees in the same way.

Best practice guidelines

Organisations are recognising the benefits of using the most talented people regardless of race, sex, age, family status or other conditions. This goes beyond equal opportunities.

- It means that an organisation reflects the community in its diversity and is better able to provide relevant goods and services, as well as develop links with the community.
- Effective policies on discrimination prevent the organisation being liable for compensation through industrial tribunals.
- Organisations should check their diversity/equal opportunities policies and practice regularly to ensure all personnel practices are free from bias.
- Regular monitoring of the composition of the workforce should show anomalies, and action can be taken.
- Policies should be published inside and externally – through job adverts, for example.
- Managers and staff may need to be trained in cultural awareness.
- Selection criteria should be reviewed to ensure they do not contain unnecessary qualifications or requirements. Overseas qualifications, for instance, can easily be checked and should not be assumed to be inferior.
- Job adverts are more likely to ensure fair employment than word of mouth.
- Keep records for all stages of recruitment and promotion so that lack of bias can be proved. Record the ethnic origin of all applicants for jobs and promotion.
- Organisations need to be flexible when it comes to religious needs.
- Special help can be given to ethnic minorities to train and encourage them for jobs where they are under-represented.
- Make sure the organisation's harassment policy covers racial harassment.
- Make sure that everyone knows that discrimination will not be tolerated.
- Monitor progress, adapt policies and practices accordingly, and publicise success.

- The above information is from Management Factsheets – *Racial Discrimination*, produced by the Industrial Society. See page 41 for address details.

Racism and xenophobia in English football

Information from Kick It Out

Introduction: football hooliganism and racism

There is a clear distinction to be made between football hooliganism and racism in the game. Whilst both problems are rooted deep in local cultures and the political history of Britain differing factors bring about these very distinct problems.

Hooliganism is essentially a problem of violence, often pre-organised, between groups of fans. Racism has found expression in the national sport as a result of the attitudes and views of supporters and the attitudes and practices of those involved in running the game.

A link between the two problems exists in so far as expressions of racialism and racial prejudice have become the common language of hooliganism, particularly for England supporters abroad, and in so doing it offers an easily subscribed-to ideological accompaniment to the culture of drunkenness and disorder.

Because of this link a rise in the problems of hooliganism results in an increase in the most easily identified forms of visible racism in and around stadiums.

Racism within the national sport

Abuse, chanting and harassment of a racist nature have a long historical relationship with football. Only a few years ago it was difficult to attend a football match without being offended by the sound of casually

expressed racial insults. These insults were most often directed at black players on the field of play or ethnic minorities at large, regardless of their actual presence in football stadiums.

Whilst the situation now is far better than it has ever been, it is our view that the problem persists at levels of intensity rarely acknowledged. The change in the situation can be characterised as a lowering of the volume.

This new situation can be attributed to a number of factors including the development of anti-racist initiatives, general developments in the game such as all-seater stadiums, and legislation, although concerns remain about the lack of enforcement.

But despite this comparative sea change in attitudes, incidents at a number of grounds last season provide examples of the sorts of problems that are recurring. These examples are just three of the many incidents reported to us.

Coventry City

At Highfield Road on October 16th 1999 during Coventry City's Premier League match with Newcastle United a large section of the Newcastle support took up the chant of 'You're a town full of Pakis' as a means of insulting the Coventry fans. The chant was taken up following an incident involving the Coventry striker Yussouf Chippo and Newcastle defender Warren Barton which resulted in the sending-off of Barton. Eyewitnesses report that the chant could be heard around the stadium and involved several thousand people. Despite the fact that both Coventry City and Newcastle pledged to look at video evidence and identify perpetrators no action was taken.

Hull City

Third Division Hull last season witnessed racial abuse directed at the club's own black players and accompanied by the singing of 'No Surrender to the IRA' and other pro-loyalist chants. Members of far-right parties were reported to have been gathering support in local pubs before and after games.

The *Hull Daily Mail* commented: 'Sectarian divisions in Northern Ireland have nothing to do with supporting Hull City. Hull City and its true supporters must do everything they can to stamp out any racism and sectarianism in their midst. It cannot be tolerated.'

Nevertheless, supporters raising public objection to the chanting were singled out and threatened at matches.

Sunderland

On February 5th during the North-East derby between Sunderland and Newcastle a section of the Sunderland fans involving several hundred people sang 'You're a team full of niggers'. Sunderland fielded only one black player last season, a Honduran international, who made periodic performances for the team, whilst Newcastle fielded a number of black players over the season.

It's often the case that the more high profile and important the match the greater the likelihood that sections of England fans will take up racist chants

---

The *Sunderland Echo* reported that members of the fascist Combat 18 from both clubs had met up in a local pub after the game.

The incidents above are not isolated occurrences but illustrate situations that Kick It Out believes occur several times throughout a season. This feeling is backed up by large numbers of supporters who continue to raise similar concerns. Two surveys of football supporters over the past year have quantified these concerns.

A survey of a panel of football supporters conducted by the Duckhams Fans View organisation found that 72% of respondents had witnessed abuse of black players over the course of last season. 65% of the same group identified racism as the most important issue facing the game. Whilst the panel members surveyed are by their very presence on a panel likely to be amongst the most enlightened of supporters familiar with the issue, another more general survey reinforces the argument.

The annual Sir Norman Chester Centre survey of season-ticket holders of 1998-99 shows that over a quarter (26%) of Premier League supporters witnessed racist abuse aimed at spectators or black players. In the Football League 32% of season-ticket holders witnessed similar abuse. At individual clubs 39% of one set of Premier League supporters reported hearing racial abuse whilst among Football League clubs 62% of one set of fans reported abuse.

Racism, xenophobia and the national team

Displays of racism and xenophobia amongst followers of the England team are common.

During the recent France v England friendly at the Stade de France in Paris (2 September 2000) England supporters took up a familiar pattern of support.

Alongside racial abuse of their own black players, much of it directed at Andrew Cole, chants such as 'Stand up if you hate the Turks', 'I'd rather be a Paki than a Turk' were widely taken up.

The chants came from the section of the ground where the

majority of England supporters were seated through the England Members' Club, the official Football Association membership scheme providing England tickets.

In 1984 England managed a famous 2-0 victory over Brazil. The first win against the Brazilians for 28 years. It was due in large part to a goal by the young John Barnes, later described by Jimmy Greaves as 'the greatest goal scored in an English shirt'.

For Barnes though the experience was tainted by an incident on the long flight back. He was approached by a clutch of supporters on the same plane as the team who told him his goal did not count because, as a black, he could not represent their national side. In their eyes, they said, the score had been 1-0.

International tournaments held in Europe, be they European Championships or World Cups, will see ugly outbursts of racism and xenophobia from English fans. It's often the case that the more high profile and important the match the greater the likelihood that sections of England fans will take up racist chants.

During Euro 2000 the songs and chants of many England fans represented the most potent form of popular racism and extreme nationalism. 'I'd rather be a Paki than a Turk', 'No Surrender to the IRA' and 'Two World Wars and a World Cup' were amongst the most frequently heard chants outside bars, inside stadiums and at other public places such as airports.

These chants are incongruous and contradictory, revealing a centre-ground where the far-right have been successful in setting the agenda.

'Two World Wars and a World Cup', for example, is a taunt aimed at Germany, England's biggest footballing rivals. The fact that the chant is usually uttered whilst giving a Sieg Heil salute offers an unsettling perspective on the reasons the wars were fought.

The 'No Surrender to the IRA' chant is often blithely taken up by many inside and outside of stadiums. As in Hull it is sometimes accompanied by other pro-loyalist chants.

'There's no racism in football . . .

. . . It was dealt with twenty years ago.'

So said a determined local football administrator last year. Sadly, he was wrong. Across the country racist attacks in amateur football are a weekly occurrence for teams from Black communities of African, African-Caribbean and Asian origin.

Even a very quick chat to local footballers reveals a deep-rooted problem that shows very little signs of abating. For some reason it's seen as legitimate to racially abuse, harass and attack players on a football pitch. 'It's part and parcel of the game' is a commonly heard excuse, as young players are being put off by the sheer intensity of the problems they face.

Effective solutions exist but are not being applied consistently across the country. On the field of play, the laws of the game have been amended to include racist abuse as a sending-off offence. Off it, local authorities can ban teams who are known racists from using their pitches and facilities, local disciplinary committees can apply the harshest measures and the police can arrest and press charges.

In professional football, despite real progress having been made, racism still exists. Some concerned fans have even pointed to a rise in racist chanting and abuse in stadiums over the past season.

A recent survey of a national panel of football supporters revealed that 72% of respondents had witnessed abuse of black players because of the colour of their skin. A previous survey had found that over 65% of those sampled had felt racism to be the most important issue facing the game. These findings support academic research that only 1% of supporters at live matches across the country are non-white.

Many more clubs are now working with the campaign to ensure they are part of the growing numbers prepared to take steps to deal with the problem. It's clear that in both the amateur and professional game action is possible. It's simply a question of will.

• The above information is from the *Kick It Out* Newsletter produced by Kick It Out. See page 41 for address details.

© *Kick It Out*

Designed to draw on populist consensus on the politics of Northern Ireland the chant also lends itself as a shorthand reference to the spirit of Englishness abroad, a determination not to give in, to fight on – No Surrender.

Events at the end of last season which resulted in two Leeds United supporters being killed whilst in

Istanbul and violence between Arsenal and Galatasaray supporters before the UEFA Cup final, have resulted in Turkish football fans, and Turks in general, being identified as the new enemy of English football supporters.

The popular expression of this hatred during Euro 2000 came in the form of the chant 'I'd rather be a Paki than a Turk' which was heard wherever England fans had gathered outside bars and pubs before and after games.

In the lexicon of football chants 'Pakis' have gradually become the measure of undesirability against which all-comers are judged. It is common throughout the football year to hear supporters from rival domestic teams singing similar songs whilst substituting the references to

'Turks' with the name of their most hated rivals. So for example in Sheffield, Sheffield Wednesday supporters abuse Sheffield United supporters by singing 'I'd rather be a Paki than a Blade'.

The campaign's plans for the forthcoming season

Having discussed possible problems during the season Kick It Out is planning a number of new initiatives to ensure our message is heard more closely. These plans, many of which are already being implemented, include:

- A standard package of anti-racist measures that clubs will be asked to deliver inside stadiums. This will sit alongside further guidance on what we expect clubs to be doing to challenge racism;
- A new freephone advice number has been set up (0800 169 9414) to encourage fans to report problems to us, directly;
- We will be asking the Football Association to hold anti-racist activities at England games over the coming year;
- A training programme aimed at increasing awareness amongst stewards to ensure problems are dealt with effectively inside stadiums;
- New publicity materials targeted at supporters who have not previously heeded anti-racist messages are being launched;
- We will be developing a closer working relationship with players and managers.

• The above information is from *Racism and Xenophobia in English football* – a paper for the Secretary of State for the Home Office, produced by Kick It Out. See page 41 for address details.

© *Kick It Out*

This misguided campaign for Asians to play football

Soccer is sometimes shamefully racist. But let's not get silly

Nobody who has ever been within spitting distance (and too often that's the phrase) of a Premier League stadium can have any doubt that racism is a cruel thorn in football's flesh. Despite valiant efforts to combat it, a long story by Rob Hughes in the *International Herald Tribune* shows how how far there is to go.

More curious, and more perplexing, is something discussed in that story. Not a single 'Asian' – I'll come back to that word – plays in the Premier League at present, and this has disquieted some in the game. The Football Supporters' Association is funding 13 projects to remedy this supposed deficiency, among them the 'Asians in Football' scheme associated with West Ham and run by Mick King, an East End social worker, which has conducted more than a thousand coaching sessions for more than 18,000 participants over the past year.

This actually raises a more complex subject than the coaches realise. Whether any ethnic group should be excluded from a sport is a question which answers itself. But is there any reason why a particular group should be encouraged – or

By Geoffrey Wheatcroft

merely expected – to play any particular sport?

To an extent which would have startled the 19th-century Oxford undergraduates who codified Association Football, this sport has become the worldwide obsession of mankind at the beginning of the third millennium. Alas, as Hughes says, a global sport now reflects global intolerance in all its forms. This is shamefully true throughout Europe. Black footballers have been jeered at (to jungle noises) in Hungary, and attacked in Germany.

In Italy there has been racial

violence on the pitch, while Emile Heskey was disgustingly abused by the crowd when England played a 'friendly' in Turin last November. And when Sturm Graz were beaten by our own champions recently, the club chairman Hannes Kartnig – who sounds a true Austrian of the old school – said on television: 'We lost because we played against Manchester United – not against any *Negermannschaft*' ('nigger team').

Not that we are in a strong position to scold. Anyone will know what I mean who has listened to the Rangers and Celtic crowds chanting their sectarian hatreds, or seen Leeds fans throwing bananas at black players, or been at Highbury when Tottenham were playing there, and heard the Gunners' fans singing: 'I never felt more like gassing the Jews/ When Tottenham win and Arsenal lose.' That piece of cheeky Cockney wit was one of the reasons I stopped going to football matches.

One thing that can be said on the other hand is that our football teams themselves are not run on racist lines. From Third Division up to national England team, they are visibly 'non-white'. Jean-Marie Le Pen thought the equally multiracial

French team which won the World Cup in 1998 and Euro 2000 was 'not worthy' of representing France. Only a small knot of bigots would dare say that our football and rugby teams are unworthy for that reason.

It's true that these teams don't precisely mirror the ethnic composition of the country, but hard to see why they ought to, as long as they are chosen on merit, as teams weren't in Nazi Germany or apartheid South Africa. Professional sport does operate on merit and the free market really works, not least against racism.

Clubs want to win. Manchester United and Lancashire and St Helens are not going to turn away a match-winning player because of the colour of his skin or his name – and that goes when the player is brown-skinned and called Singh or Patel. Nor does anyone that I know of suggest that they do.

And so if there is no 'Asian' footballer at a high level, does that actually matter in itself? Even the word 'Asian' is distasteful and fatuous. It is never used in this country to describe a Turk, Uzbeki or Cambodian, though it covers them geographically, but then the explanation for this foolish usage is historical. 'Asian' is shorthand for 'of Indian-subcontinental birth or origin'. Sixty years ago, before partition and the Mountbatten massacres, anyone from Karachi or Dhaka as well as from Bombay or Calcutta could be called Indian.

If 'Asian' is irritating enough when used of people actually born in the subcontinent, it is repellent cant when used of our fellow-citizens. Asia is a large continent a long way away. Asians are born there. Someone born in this country is British, and European. Keith Vaz's claim that he is a 'leading member of the Asian community' would be obnoxious even if it weren't an excuse for sucking up to shady millionaire arms-dealers.

It's true that these teams don't precisely mirror the ethnic composition of the country, but hard to see why they ought to, as long as they are chosen on merit

---

As for the exiguity of 'Asian' footballers, racists might say that this is because 'Asians' are puny or timid; professional anti-racists will say that it is because of prejudice. I would say that it is quite obviously because of historical and cultural reasons. 'Vive la différence' is a fruitful slogan in sport; and it's just as cheering that good little ones can beat big ones. For generations past, New Zealand has produced world-beating rugby teams, and Argentine football teams have often beaten Brazil which has five times the population. Indonesia and Malaysia can't be called little, but mere numbers cannot explain the fact that between them they could beat the rest of the world at badminton, as Pakistan could at squash.

And there is a non-racist tradition in sport, as authentic in its way as the loathly spoor of racism. One of the happier memories from the days when the sun never set on the British empire and we held dominion over palm and pine is of 'Ranji', 'Duleep' and the Nawab of Pataudi playing cricket for England (albeit with somewhat flimsy national qualifications). And one of the better things about English cricket today is the 'Asians' playing here. Mick King might have noticed that Mark Ramprakash has played for England, Min Patel might yet, and Nasser Hussain captains the national side.

Not only does anti-racism sometimes painfully mimic the language of racism (the uses of 'black' as well as 'Asian' are worth de-constructing in this context), but anti-racists too often trip over their own logic. If it is wrong that 'Asians' are represented in football so far below their proportion in the population, then why is it right that black people (of Afro-Caribbean origin) are represented so much above?

Racism in sport should be stamped out: real racism, not imaginary. To test where it exists or not, you must imagine a project called 'Black athletes in football'. Nothing could sound odder – unless it were 'Asians in cricket'. Mick King's heart is in the right place, but he would do better to go with the cultural flow and encourage as many 'Asians' as possible to play cricket. One of them might even turn out to be the great spinner we desperately need.

Let's beat racism

Information from ChildLine

What is racism?

'My mum said she doesn't really mind me having black friends, but she would draw the line at me going out with "one of them".'

'I hate the way people talk to me as though I can't speak English, just because my parents are Chinese.'

'I can't walk down the street with my boyfriend because our families wouldn't approve of us going out together.'

The facts:

- 79% of black Caribbean boys and 70% of Asian boys and girls said they'd been picked on at school.
- Young people from ethnic minorities are almost twice as likely to be unemployed as their white counterparts.
- 16- 25-year-olds were the offenders in 53% of racially motivated incidents against Asians and 36% of those against black Caribbeans.
- 60% of British people said in a survey they would marry people from another race, or be happy for their son or daughter to do the same.

ChildLine

0800 1111

Racists are:

Shallow because they won't look at another person's character or personality – they will only see as far as skin colour, style of dress or the language spoken.

Quick to judge those who are different from themselves.

Dangerous because they spread hatred and violence through their beliefs. They'd rather see divides in our society than hope that everyone could live in peace together.

Are you being bullied OR discriminated against?

10 points to help

1. Stop taking the abuse

You don't have to accept this sort of hassle. Everyone has a right to live happily and free from discrimination, no matter what their nationality or race.

2. Accept that you're not the one with the problem

Your self-esteem may have taken a knock if you're having a hard time, but the thing you have to remember is that you are not the one to have caused the problem.

3. Tell someone what's happening to you

You don't have to suffer in silence. Think who's the best person to talk to about what's happening. Schools, police and employers have a responsibility to protect you. Other parts of your life will suffer if you keep silent. If the problem is at school, your work might deteriorate. Speak up now before the problem takes over. Why not try having a word with a ChildLine counsellor first to try out what you would like to say?

4. Go for a team effort

Get other people involved in tackling the problem – perhaps you could

start an anti-racism project or newsletter at your school or youth group and invite an anti-racist speaker along. Or set up a discussion group to talk about relevant issues and see what you can do to help in your area.

5. Make people take you seriously
If you are going to alert someone to the fact that you're being threatened, abused or bullied, then do it properly. You have to be prepared to get across just how it is affecting your well-being.

6. Keep some evidence of what's happening (a diary of events, for example)
This might be useful to show others that you need help.

7. Plan what you would like to happen
Now go for it.

8. Make other parts of your life even better
Don't let racists ruin every area of your life. For example, if you're unhappy at school or work, then make sure you make up for the bad times by enjoying yourself at home or with your friends.

9. Keep safe and aware
You can't spend your life looking over your shoulder, but it pays to be aware of dangers. Stick with groups of friends if you feel vulnerable.

10. Never give up!
You might not be able to tackle racism by yourself. Seek out support and accept help where you can.

How can you help a friend or neighbour?
You may not be the person being persecuted, but there are lots of things you can do to help a friend or neighbour who is the victim of racial discrimination . . .

Listen
Being the subject of racist abuse damages self-esteem. You can help by listening to your friend talk about their experiences – a good way to vent anger, frustration and feelings of injustice.

Take them seriously
They may feel like no one is taking their problem to heart. Make sure they know you're there to sympathise and be prepared to help sort out the situation.

Try to get help
If your friend is scared to get help, or wary of being branded 'a grass', then it might take a third party to alert attention to the problem.

Don't join the racists
It's hard to make a stand, even if you're not the victim. You may be worried that you'll be next. But what you shouldn't do is join in, hoping that if you share their views you'll be safe. Report incidents to someone else who can act on your behalf if you don't want to get directly involved.

© ChildLine

Action being taken to tackle racial harassment

Information from the Joseph Rowntree Foundation

Background
The Macpherson report into the death of Stephen Lawrence drew attention to the extent and seriousness of racial attacks. But racial harassment is not new. In the 1980s, Select Committees and the Home Office brought the problem to the notice of the police, local authorities, social landlords and independent campaigning and advocacy groups. Since then, many suggestions of good practice have been made by a range of statutory and independent groups. For this study, the researchers interviewed 250 practitioners working with victims or perpetrators of racial harassment in 67 local authority areas. The interviewees were mainly drawn from the police, local authority community safety units, social landlords, specialist and voluntary organisations.

The respondents were asked to describe the types of action being taken by their own organisation and by other agencies working in the area to tackle racial harassment. The questions concentrated on five main areas:
- multi-agency working;
- reporting and recording;
- support for victims;
- action against perpetrators;
- training.

The extent of racial harassment
The number of incidents reported varied widely between local authority areas. In eight areas, the number of recorded incidents of racial harassment from all agencies was less than 100. At the other end of the range, 13 areas reported more than 1,000 incidents in the last year. Organisations in the London Borough of Newham had received most reports – 2,134 – during 1999-2000.

The agencies in the survey had received a total of 41,925 reports of racial harassment between April 1999 and March 2000, a mean of 635 reports per area (in one borough, no agency was able to give a recent figure for the number of reports). This compares with a total of just over 23,000 racial incidents recorded by all British police forces during the year.

These figures refer only to reports of racial harassment, not the actual level of harassment. Almost all the organisations in the sample had seen a significant increase in cases reported to them since the Stephen Lawrence Inquiry; many police divisions reported a doubling of reports during 1999-2000. But several respondents felt that under-reporting (or under-recording by the agencies themselves) was still a significant problem for some groups, such as refugees.

Multi-agency working

Multi-agency groups or panels have been set up in 53 (78 per cent) of the areas. In some areas the multi-agency forum's work was restricted to a strategic role, usually the development of joint policies and the monitoring of local trends in reporting.

Often a separate panel of practitioners from key agencies considered individual cases, using 'depersonalised' (anonymous) data on victims. These casework forums existed in 34 (51 per cent) of the areas in the survey.

Interviewees frequently raised resources as a problem for the multi-agency forums. In addition, in some areas there were tensions between partner organisations. However, there were also examples where the partners co-operated efficiently. For example, the Glasgow case group had met within hours to co-ordinate the support and rehousing of victims in particularly serious cases.

Reporting and recording

Third-party reporting centres collecting reports and passing them on to key agencies had been developed in 37 areas (55 per cent). They included advice centres, places of worship, community associations, and some-times also doctors' surgeries and public buildings (such as libraries and schools). Staff in independent centres needed training, which required time and money. Some interviewees expressed dis-appointment that third-party centres did not generate large numbers of extra reports, while others felt that their value lay in the fact that people using them were unlikely to report to other agencies.

Common reporting forms were generally viewed positively in the 39 areas (58 per cent) where they were in use, although some agencies were concerned about the potential breach of confidentiality involved in passing information to another organisation. Most areas using common reporting forms stored the data on a central database for monitoring purposes, often maintained by staff at the local racial equality council or a specialist agency.

Support for victims

In most of the areas the police or the housing department were willing to provide *alarms* for vulnerable tenants experiencing harassment or living in high-risk areas. These were usually linked to the local council's twenty-four-hour careline for older and disabled residents. The consensus among practitioners was that alarms provided a high degree of reassurance to frightened tenants.

Less than a third of areas had a *twenty-four-hour helpline* that could give advice to victims of racial harassment. In many other districts the reporting lines were only answered during office hours, with an answerphone taking messages at other times.

Respondents stated that *counselling* was available in a third of the areas. But few areas have in-depth counselling by trained staff familiar with racial harassment. In most other areas 'providing advice', rather than 'counselling', would be a more accurate description.

Most housing departments had made *security improvements* to individual properties. The most common ones were stronger locks and doors. Fencing and improved lighting around the property were also mentioned by several housing managers. More extreme forms of

'target hardening', such as fireproof letterboxes, were less common.

Council housing departments and social landlords were divided about their approach to *rehousing* victims. In some areas housing managers were reluctant to grant transfers, arguing that it allowed perpetrators to drive tenants from 'white' estates. Other councils considered the victim's security to be paramount and offered transfers (or temporary rehousing) whenever it was requested. Twenty-seven of the councils in the survey had rehoused a total of 138 households because of racial incidents. Given the high number of reports of racial harassment, such a low level of transfers strongly suggests that fears expressed by some housing staff that tenants may claim harassment to jump the transfer queue are un-founded.

Action against perpetrators

Social landlords in the survey had taken *possession proceedings* in a total of 124 cases because of anti-social behaviour that had a racial element. Their main criticism of the procedure was that it was too slow, although there was a feeling that judges had become more prepared to grant possession in racial harassment cases than in the past. In general, housing managers felt that suspended orders or threats of eviction had the desired deterrent effect on racist tenants.

Recent figures on *criminal prosecutions* were available in 35 of the areas. In total, 2,451 had been brought in these areas in the last year (an average of 79 prosecutions per borough). Around 10 to 15 per cent of reports to the police ended in a prosecution. Some police officers felt that the Crown Prosecution Service did not always stress the racial element enough in prosecutions for racial harassment.

Anti-social behaviour orders (ASBOs) had only been taken out against racial perpetrators in three of the areas. Applying for an order was often seen as a time-consuming and uncertain process; for example, one council's attempt to obtain an order for racial harassment was thwarted when the perpetrator changed his address.

Twenty-seven local authorities had taken out 124 *injunctions* against perpetrators of racial harassment; an average of 5 injunctions in each of these boroughs. In general, injunctions were seen as a quick way to take action in serious cases. Where councils were not using injunctions, housing officers often attributed this to excessive caution by legal staff. Questions were also raised by some respondents about the training and competence of housing managers in the use of injunctions.

Since the organisations in the survey had received over 40,000 reports of racial harassment, legal action was being taken in only a small proportion of cases. Victims and witnesses were said to be reluctant to make statements for fear of reprisals. Interviewees reported that attempts to overcome this with *professional witnesses* had generally been expensive with disappointing results, while non-legal solutions such as *mediation* were often seen as inappropriate in racial harassment cases.

A few areas were developing schemes to change the *behaviour* of perpetrators. Examples included work with racist offenders by probation officers and community justice schemes for young offenders. However, programmes of this sort were rare.

Training
In 50 areas (75 per cent) front-line staff in at least one of the organisations contacted had received specific training on racial harassment.

Housing officers and police staff were most likely to receive some training, although this was often rather limited and some police officers expressed concern at the slow implementation of force-wide training schemes.

Innovative practice
Examples of innovative practice from the four case study areas included:
- Single Regeneration Budget funding for casework and co-ordination in Ipswich;
- work with young people in sports clubs in Leeds;
- lay advisers to the police in racist incidents panels in Leeds;

- restorative justice in racial harassment cases in Reading. A trained police officer chairs a meeting between the perpetrator and the victims, confronting the offender with the impact of the harassment and agreeing on the amends to be made. The 'restorative caution' can be taken into account if the perpetrator reoffends;
- self-help groups for victims of racial harassment in Reading;
- witness mobility scheme in Waltham Forest;
- use of specialist agency in Waltham Forest;
- specialist lawyer in Waltham Forest.

In other areas, examples of innovative practice included:
- public awareness campaigns against race and hate crimes;
- cable TV to encourage reporting;
- one-stop shops and information hotlines for reporting racist incidents;
- mapping racist incidents;
- counselling for victims;
- home/school liaison;
- anti-racial harassment worker in private sector housing unit;
- proposed refuge and advice centre for victims;
- probation and police working to change the offending behaviour of perpetrators;
- anti-social behaviour orders;
- mediation.

Conclusions
This research investigated the type of action being taken in the boroughs. A key theme that emerged from the interviews was the need to evaluate the effectiveness of action. In particular, there appears to be a case for:
- local crime surveys to establish the true level of racial harassment, as opposed to reported incidents, as well as action research to improve reporting and recording;
- evaluation of third-party reporting centres – for example, do victims get the practical and emotional support they need after reporting incidents?
- research into the long-term impact of racial harassment for victims and guidance to agencies on the emotional and social impact of racial harassment on the lives of the victims and the development of effective counselling services;
- guidance to social landlords on the rehousing of victims and the provision of other places of safety for victims;
- evaluation of the action taken against perpetrators looking especially at why civil legal remedies are not more frequently used and at newer approaches that attempt to challenge the attitudes and behaviour of perpetrators.

Policy implications

The report suggests consideration of the following innovations in national approaches to dealing with racial harassment:

- A national reporting and helpline for victims of racial harassment;
- A national network of specialist support services;
- National standards of training and competence for front-line staff in the police, local authorities and social landlords;
- A national programme of positive work to change the offending behaviour of perpetrators.

About the study

In-depth semi-structured interviews were conducted with more than 250 practitioners working with victims or perpetrators of racial harassment in 67 local authority areas.

The local authority areas were selected because they had the highest numbers of black and minority ethnic inhabitants at the 1991 Census. Because of this, it may be dangerous to extrapolate the findings to other parts of Britain.

In addition, more detailed case studies have been written up of four local authority areas where most of the existing recommended good practice was being followed – Ipswich, Leeds, Reading and Waltham Forest. A number of examples of innovative practice from elsewhere were also collected. A directory of contacts and action drawn from the survey, along with a discussion forum, legal guidance, learning materials and case studies of innovative practice, will be available to agencies dealing with racial harassment on a password-protected website from early 2001 – www.RaceActionNet.co.uk.

- The above information is from the Joseph Rowntree Foundation, see page 41 for their address details.

© Joseph Rowntree Foundation

Racist bullying

Can we stop it?

Racism takes many forms. People can stereotype and discriminate against people merely because of the colour of their skin. But the more brutal end of racism includes attacks and bullying.

Here Tamara Wilder from Victim Support gives some advice on what to do about racist bullying.

We all know racism exists in this country, we may not like it, but it's a fact of life that most of us will have experienced it at some time or other.

Racism isn't just a case of black versus white, it is much deeper than that. It might be the group of white kids targeting the lone black one. It might be because someone is Asian, Chinese, Irish or Jewish. It might be because they speak a different language or have a different skin colour.

The bad news is that it's not going to go away quickly. The good news is that there are things you can do to help fight the racists and learn to stand proud.

If you think you are being victimised due to a racist attack then tell someone as soon as possible about the nature of the bullying. Try talking to a teacher or parent if you can. If there is no one you feel comfortable talking to there are a number of organisations that will listen to your concerns in confidence and can offer practical advice about how to cope.

Here are some ways in which you can deal with this kind of abuse:

You don't have to accept this sort of discrimination

We all have a right to live without this sort of hassle regardless of race or nationality. So don't accept it, do something about it.

Realise that it's not you with a problem

It's hard to stand tall and walk away from bullies, your self-confidence has taken a battering, but it's not your fault and you haven't done anything to make people torment you in this way.

We all know racism exists in this country, we may not like it but it's a fact of life that most of us will have experienced it at sometime or other

Tell someone what is happening to you

Don't suffer in silence. Telling someone is the first step in sorting the problem out. Find someone you can trust before the problem spirals out of control. Speaking to someone at Victim Support can help put the problem into perspective as they are removed from your own situation.

Group help

Is there a group of you being targeted? Try and raise the issue at school in the school magazine or set up a discussion in RE or General Studies. Perhaps your local Victim Support has an 'anti-racism road-show' which can come into your school to address the problems of racism.

Keep a note of what is happening

This might be useful to show others what is happening to you and to prove it if necessary.

Don't rise to the problem

There is little point answering back to racists. It will only incite them to make the taunts worse and more often. Instead, try to seek help and talk about the issue.

Be aware

You can't spend your life worrying about racists but do be careful not to take unnecessary risks. Try not to walk about on your own where you know people who taunt you will be.

Stay confident

Don't let racists ruin your life, this isn't easy but it is important to make sure you keep your self-esteem. You might not be a ringer for Posh Spice or David Beckham but learning to love yourself makes you feel and look more confident.

Have a plan

Think about how you want this to stop, what you intend to do and who is going to help you.

Don't give up

It may well stop if you don't let it bother you. Keep talking about it and telling people who can help you and try not to let it get you down!

Victim Supportline: 0845 3030900. 9am – 9pm weekdays. 9am – 7pm weekends.

• The above information is from a Video Resource Pack produced by Show Racism the Red Card. See page 41 for address details.

Teaching tolerance in the classroom

Within two years schools will be required to teach pupils about other cultures and faiths. But, as *Connections* reports, many educationalists are already taking the initiative against racism.

In his report on the police investigation of the murder of Stephen Lawrence, Sir William Macpherson suggested that education could play a major role in preventing racism. He proposed that the national curriculum should be revised to 'value diversity'. And he asked all LEAs and school governments to implement strategies against racism, with all incidents being monitored and reported. He also suggested that inspections by OFSTED, the Office for Standards in Education, should measure how well anti-racist strategies were working.

Macpherson warned of the presence of 'institutional racism' – the collective failure to provide a service to people because of their race. This sort of institutionalised racism, which has been condemned by the government, is something which can affect schools as much as other organisations.

It is now almost two years since the report saw the light of day. But the questions remain: Are schools taking steps to challenge racism and to promote cultural and ethnic diversity? If they are, are they being effective? And how are the key national agencies fulfilling their responsibility?

The government, in its response to the Stephen Lawrence Inquiry, suggested that a new subject – citizenship – could meet the objective of valuing diversity. From 2002, school pupils between the ages of 11 and 16 (key stages 3 and 4) will have to study citizenship. There are two ways this can be done: either as part of existing subjects, such as history, or as a completely new subject.

Teaching materials are currently being prepared by the government-funded Qualifications and Curriculum Authority (QCA), although schools will be free to use their own. John Keast, who is in charge of the citizenship project for the QCA, explained: 'What we're doing is very hard-edged, with emphasis on giving pupils knowledge about other ethnic groups.'

Sarah Maclean, who is the team leader of the Department for Education and Employment's citizenship project, explained that teachers would be recruited specifically to teach citizenship, including anti-

racism. And there might even be a new 'short course' GCSE in citizenship. The DfEE will hold regional conferences to explain to teachers and LEAs what the new subject involves.

Curriculum

The CRE has reservations about teaching citizenship as a 'single subject'. Rather than locate issues relating to racism and cultural and ethnic diversity within one subject area, it would prefer that racial equality should be addressed across the curriculum.

In its standard for racial equality, *Learning for All*, which was distributed to all schools, the CRE suggested that racial equality objectives should be 'built into all programmes of work'. The skills and expertise of local ethnic minority communities should be used within the curriculum and tasks should be set which 'raise awareness of different cultures and challenge prejudices and stereotypes'.

Schools wishing to take this approach will be able to use research being done by the QCA, which is currently making efforts to identify examples of good racial equality practice in all areas of the curriculum. Over the next year the QCA will also be setting up a website with examples of good practice.

Citizenship will only be taught to older children. For children under 11 (key stages 1 and 2), racism and racial equality will be dealt with as part of Personal Social and Health Education, a subject which is not compulsory. The DfEE suggests that OFSTED would take a dim view of schools which ignore this subject; however, the fact remains that primary schools will not be required to tackle racism or promote diversity as part of the curriculum.

There have been some conspicuous failures in addressing racism: most notably by OFSTED, which was severely criticised in a CRE report. The report, by educationalists Audrey Osler and Marlene Morrison, showed that OFSTED inspectors failed to inspect and report racism directly in school inspection reports. Inspectors often lacked the experience and motivation to look at racial issues properly.

Despite these criticisms, senior management at OFSTED have refused to review the organisation's methods of working. Nor will they do any independent research of their own.

Local education authorities can also play a role in opposing discrimination. According to the CRE's standard, *Learning for All*, LEAs and schools should work closely together to deal with racist incidents and to evaluate policies.

Some LEAs have won praise for their efforts. Last year Hertfordshire introduced a system which enables parents who feel that their children are experiencing racism to go directly to the LEA. All parents are given a contact number for an LEA officer who can investigate complaints of racial harassment.

Jan Hardy, head of the ethnic minority curriculum support service at Hertfordshire LEA, said: 'Every member of staff has been briefed on racism. Every school has to produce an action plan. All racist incidents are investigated. Previously we only looked at racial incidents which involved physical assaults or which involved the police.'

Awareness

Since 1996 more than 1,000 Hertfordshire teachers have had racism-awareness courses. And schools have to survey pupils to find out whether they perceive racism as a problem. 'This sort of dialogue can be very revealing to teachers,' said Hardy.

The LEA has made extensive use of Ethnic Minority Achievement Grants, which have been used to pay, among other things, for mentoring sessions. Mentors are often people who were themselves unruly pupils, but went on to build successful careers. They can teach strategies for avoiding problems and

---

'What we're doing is very hard-edged, with emphasis on giving pupils knowledge about other ethnic groups'

---

coping with pressures. Hertfordshire claims that such initiatives have reduced exclusions. However, some critics have derided the ethnic minority grants as an elaborate way of diverting money away from teaching.

Research by the Children's Legal Centre has shown that it is important for all schools, even those with relatively small numbers of ethnic minority children, to take racism seriously. Some of the worst racism can occur in predominantly white areas. Families in this position feel more isolated than those where there is a larger ethnic minority community.

Schools around the country are taking their own initiatives. The Henry Compton secondary school in Fulham was, until 1996, a failing school. Since then standards have improved greatly and new anti-racist initiatives have been adopted, such as language support and special teaching for the travelling community.

Deputy head Robert Doyle explained: 'We work hard on racial awareness. The school has done a lot of work with Travellers – particularly from eastern Europe. As a result it has become a magnet for Kosovans, who know that their children will get a sympathetic education.'

Teaching unions have issued guidelines urging schools to pay particular attention to such things as dress requirements, dietary restrictions or religious holidays and holding anti-racist training seminars. Unions are asking LEAs for extra funds to pay teachers for undertaking anti-racist training and monitoring.

Key national agencies and LEAs have an important role in encouraging, supporting and guiding schools to address racial equality issues. Schools are not always skilled or equipped to deal with issues. Only by linking the work done by schools to the efforts of officials can racism genuinely be confronted.

● The above information is an extract from *Connections*, the quarterly magazine produced by the Commission for Racial Equality (CRE). See page 41 for address details
© *Commission for Racial Equality (CRE)*

Black culture 'holding back' boys

By Liz Lightfoot,
Education Correspondent

A leading black academic undertaking research for the Commission for Racial Equality has fuelled the row over boys' educational under-achievement by suggesting that Afro-Caribbean youth culture was partly to blame.

Tony Sewell, a lecturer in education and the author of books on the schooling of black pupils, claimed that large sections of his community were not interested in intellectual activity and that fashionable youth culture, with its interest in money and consumer goods, was now more damaging to black pupils' chances than racism. Black peer grouping and culture was propping up the sale of trainers and rap music, he told the *Telegraph* yesterday.

He gave warning that it was crossing over to white teenagers who admired it. Dr Sewell said: 'Black culture has become the dominant culture and it now affects everyone, so if the Government wants to improve standards for all boys it will have to get it right with black boys first.'

His comments came as the Government braced itself for examination statistics this week that are expected to show the gap between the achievements of girls and boys widening still further. Girls outperformed boys for the first time at A-level last week and the GCSE results to be published on Thursday are believed to show girls continuing to increase their lead over boys at 16 by gaining an even higher proportion of the top grades.

David Blunkett, the Education Secretary, yesterday released details of measures to tackle boys' underachievement but he stressed that parents and schools also had a part to play. Dr Sewell, a lecturer in education at Leeds University, has just completed an inquiry into the high level of exclusions of black pupils at a London secondary school. He is also investigating allegations,

on behalf of the CRE, that some of the staff displayed racist attitudes.

Black pupils had gained much needed self-esteem from their youth culture as it became part of the mainstream, he said. 'But that culture is not one that, for example, is interested in being a great chess player, or intellectual activity. It is actually to do with propping up a big commercial culture to do with selling trainers, selling magazines, rap music and so on.'

> *Fashionable youth culture, with its interest in money and consumer goods, was now more damaging to black pupils' chances than racism*

Dr Sewell said that racism was the main obstacle to achievement 30 years ago when he was at school but now it was youth culture. 'Black culture is driven by commercial culture which doesn't appear to be able to market trainers, CDs or mobile phones without a black image. These things are not harmful in themselves but what is dangerous is the inability of children to see that they can have this type of culture and still succeed at school. Unfortunately to be good at school is seen as nerdy and white while it's cool to be black.'

He is to publish research based on a project with inner-city youths which proved it was possible to challenge the dominant street culture by showing adolescents that they could be both cool, black and clever. His claims were immediately challenged by other leading black figures, but Trevor Phillips, the broadcaster, warned that the 'gold chains and no brains' street culture was becoming 'a new mental ghetto'.

Coming from the street, rather than holding down a job and being a father, was becoming the 'latest test of authenticity', he said. 'We are only genuinely black if we speak Jamaican, wear expensive designer clothes and reject anything that resembles formal

Britain: a racist society?

MORI asked a representative sample of 11-16-year-olds about the pervasiveness of racism today. On balance, young people do agree that Britain is a racist society (37% agree vs. 22% disagree) – however, there is no significant difference between the views of white pupils and those from black and ethnic groups.

Q. How strongly do you agree or disagree that Britain is a racist society?

	Agree	Disagree
All pupils	37%	22%
White pupils	37%	22%
Black and ethnic minority pupils	40%	21%

Source: Market & Opinion Research International (MORI)

education or scholarship.' It was a pernicious, racist trap, similar to the racist stereotypes of black men as musical, sporty and virile, he argued.

The argument was vigorously opposed, however, by Lee Jasper, who advises Ken Livingstone, the mayor of London, on race relations. 'Tony Sewell is somebody who gets attention for saying the things that well-meaning white liberals would naturally agree with.' Black youth culture should be a source of pride, he added. The problems suffered by black youth were more to do with racism in that black families were more likely to live in poor housing, be unemployed and be excluded from school.

There were many schools in inner-city areas where the white parents had sent their children elsewhere and the pupils were 99 per cent black, taught by a 99 per cent white teaching staff. 'Move these black youngsters to Chelsea or Kensington and they would become doctors and dentists like white people. The success of black culture has shown that black people can succeed at anything if you give them a chance.'

Mr Blunkett will announce today that local education authorities and Ofsted are being asked to evaluate experiments taking place in co-educational schools where boys and girls are being taught separately for some subjects to see if the practice should be extended. More vocational courses will be provided and more apprenticeships and other links to the workplace, to motivate young men.

Mr Blunkett said: 'The gap that has opened up between the sexes at school is a long-standing and international problem for which there is no quick fix but I am determined that our boys should not miss out. We have to say to young men that there will be a job at the end of it. For 20 years there has been no certainty of employment for them.'

Mr Blunkett said he was concerned over the lower achievements of Afro-Caribbean boys and their high rate of exclusion. However, their problems were mirrored by those of white working-class boys. He said: 'It appears to be to do with the culture they are living in, the low expectations they have of themselves and the low aspirations of the community around them.'

© Telegraph Group Limited, London 2000

Embracing the need to build an inclusive society

Britain must take into account the changes of the last 30 years and reimagine itself as a genuinely multicultural community

England, Scotland and Wales are at a turning point in their history. They could become narrow and inward looking, with rifts between themselves and among their regions and communities, or they could develop as a 'community of citizens and communities'.

Many customary images of Britain are England-centred – indeed southern England-centred – and leave many millions of people out of the picture.

More and more people have multiple identities – they are Welsh Europeans, Pakistani Yorkshire-women, Glaswegian Muslims, English Jews.

Diversity gives Britain important opportunities in world markets. Yet the opportunity is in danger of being squandered through racism and exclusion.

Aggressive hostility to Islam is expressed in ways unthinkable in relation to other beliefs. The state's attitude to asylum seekers sends a shiver down many spines. Stories of murders, injustices and outrages haunt many people's memories.

People in Britain have many differences, but they inhabit the same space and share the same future. All have a role in the collective project of fashioning Britain as an outward-looking, generous, inclusive society.

If Britain is to flourish, its political leaders should shape, not pander to, public opinion on issues relating to race and diversity

A state is not only a territorial and political entity, but also an 'imagined community'. A genuinely multicultural Britain urgently needs to reimagine itself.

Among other things, such reimagining must take account of the inescapable changes of the last 30 years – not only post-war migration but also devolution, globalisation, the end of empire, Britain's long-term decline as a world power, moral and cultural pluralism and closer integration with Europe.

'Community' is a tricky term. All communities are changing and all are complex, with internal diversities and disagreements. There are also many overlaps, borrowings and two-way influences – no community is or can be insulated from all others.

Hybrid cultural forms have emerged, especially in music and the arts. In this context, does 'Britishness' have a future? Some believe devolution, globalisation and the new cultural diversity have undermined it irretrievably.

The government has stated that it is committed 'to creating one

32

nation'. What values and loyalties must be shared by communities and individuals in one nation?

Most theoretical debates on such issues in Britain have been between what may be called nationalist and liberal theories of society.

Under the nationalist model, the state promotes a single national culture and expects all to assimilate it. People who do not or cannot assimilate are second-class citizens.

Under the liberal model, there is a single political culture in the public sphere, but substantial diversity in the private lives of citizens.

A third model is the pluralist one which rejects a hard and fast distinction between public and private spheres and envisages that the public realm should be continually revised to accommodate cultural diversity in society at large.

This model is to be found in multicultural societies such as Canada, Australia, Malaysia and India.

The need now is for debates between liberal and pluralist theories. Britain should develop both as a community of citizens (the liberal view) and as a community of communities (the pluralist view).

A more ceremonious form of welcome for new British citizens might help everyone reflect on the value of citizenship.

As far as racism is concerned, hostility that uses skin colour and physical appearance as markers of supposed difference does not represent the whole picture.

There is also hostility using markers connected with culture, language and religion. A distinction needs also to be drawn between overt racism and institutional racism.

Differentials in income and life-chances between black, Asian and Irish people and the rest of the population must be tackled.

Sixty per cent of people of Bangladeshi or Pakistani origin live in poverty. More than half of African-Caribbean and African people live in districts with the highest rates of unemployment.

Also, entirely independently of ethnicity, there must be progress to cut differentials in the general population between regions and neighbourhoods.

Negotiations over contested issues – for example, the content of the national curriculum, the wearing of religious clothing at work – cannot take place in an ethical vacuum. They require ground rules that provide a minimum guarantee of protection for individuals and a framework for handling conflicts of interest.

Such ground rules are provided in part by international human rights standards.

The country's criminal justice system must on the one hand deal with racist crime with the utmost vigour; on the other, it must engage in its own processes with the utmost professionalism and fairness and with the minimum of damage to wider relationships and public trust.

There is a growing body of data showing that black and Irish people are treated differentially at all stages of the criminal justice process, and that they are disproportionately likely to be imprisoned.

In education, monitoring by ethnicity is inadequate or non-existent. There are substantial inequalities affecting, in particular, pupils and students from African-Caribbean, Bangladeshi and Pakistani communities.

The cultural fabric of a society expresses ideas of who 'we' are. The media have an essential role to play.

The NHS depends . . . on the contributions of Asian, black and Irish doctors, nurses, managers and ancillary staff.

At the same time, patterns of mortality and morbidity are more serious in Asian, black and Irish communities than in the population as a whole, and there is much insensitivity in the NHS to the distinctive experiences, situations and requirements of these communities.

There are two problems with the approach to asylum and immigration by both major political parties.

First, the sense of panic the issue instils and the subjectivity with which it is discussed lead to bad law that does not work even in its own terms, giving rise to challenges both in UK courts and among international human rights bodies.

Second, it undermines Britain's development as a community of communities.

If Britain is to flourish, its political leaders should shape, not pander to, public opinion on issues relating to race and diversity.

A thoroughgoing review of religion in Britain would need to reconsider a wide range of connections between the Church of England and the state; in particular, legislation widely felt to privilege Anglicans in England over other denominations and faiths.

The Race Relations Act 1976 has had a positive effect. However, a new Equality Act is required, together with a new Equality Commission.

Furthermore, there needs to be a Human Rights Commission to promote a human rights culture, and the United Kingdom should formally declare itself to be a multicultural society.

© Guardian Newspapers Limited 2000

Public sector forced to tackle racism

Straw tackles 'official' racism

By Alan Travis, Home Affairs Editor

Jack Straw, the home secretary, will tomorrow announce new powers giving statutory force to the official campaign to tackle institutional racism in schools, hospitals, universities and across the whole public sector, including the police and prisons, the *Guardian* has learned.

From April a positive legal duty to promote good race relations and equality of opportunity will be imposed on every public body, including ministries, Whitehall departments and local government.

They will have to monitor the ethnic composition of their workforce to ensure it reflects the minority ethnic make-up of their local community.

Public bodies will have a duty to assess the impact on racial equality of proposed policies and new services. For example, if an NHS trust proposes to close, or open, a hospital it would have to publish an assessment of what impact it would have on local minority ethnic communities.

The announcement is being made by Mr Straw in a 60-page consultation paper as part of his attempt to maintain the momentum behind the government's anti-racist campaign. This weekend marks the second anniversary of the official inquiry report into the murder of the black teenager Stephen Lawrence. Mr Straw will tomorrow announce the latest progress report on the 70 recommendations by Sir William Macpherson.

Attempts by the police to tackle institutional racism have already provoked a backlash from some officers who have received the backing of William Hague and some newspapers. The decision to extend the fight right across the public sector, backed by 'legal teeth', is likely to intensify the debate.

The statutory duty to combat institutional racism will mean public organisations will have to monitor the impact of existing policies on race equality. So far public debate on this has centred on such questions as the use by police of stop and search tactics, or practices inside the prison service.

> **From April a positive legal duty to promote good race relations and equality of opportunity will be imposed on every public body**

The way councils or housing associations allocate homes, or the way schools operate their exclusion policies towards troublesome pupils, will also come under scrutiny.

The new duty will mean that an education authority or a university will have to publish an annual assessment which would not only detail the minority ethnic composition of teaching staff and others but specify levels of achievement by different ethnic groups and incidents of racial harassment.

The measures will be legally enforceable by the commission for racial equality. Official inspection bodies such as Ofsted, HM inspector of police, the chief inspector of prisons, the audit commission and the national audit office will also be able to order compliance.

The consultation paper will leave open the question of whether individual schools or the local education authority will be made the legally responsible body for tackling institutional racism. Ministers are anxious not to create a new bureaucratic paperwork burden on head teachers, or hospital administrators.

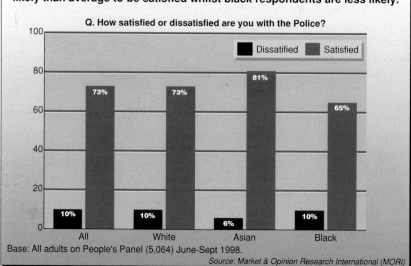

Satisfaction with the Police

Research through the Government's People's Panel shows that public satisfaction with the Police is generally very high, although there are some differences in opinion by broad ethnic group. Asian respondents are more likely than average to be satisfied whilst black respondents are less likely.

Q. How satisfied or dissatisfied are you with the Police?

- Dissatified
- Satisfied

	All	White	Asian	Black
Satisfied	73%	73%	81%	65%
Dissatified	10%	10%	6%	10%

Base: All adults on People's Panel (5,064) June-Sept 1998.
Source: Market & Opinion Research International (MORI)

Scots under fire

'Scratching the surface' with anti-racism plans

The Scottish executive has come under fire from minority ethnic groups for failing to take on board the key lessons of the Stephen Lawrence inquiry.

The criticism came as a steering group, set up by the executive in the wake of the inquiry report two years ago, outlined the progress made during the last year and made a number of recommendations for further action.

The executive accepted most of the Lawrence inquiry's 70 recommendations and unveiled an action plan in July 1999. But two key recommendations – that there should be a new independent body to investigate complaints against police, and that officers should be disciplined after retirement – were not fully backed and are still being considered.

The steering group calls for the development of performance indicators for tackling racism among police and other public sector bodies, and for steps to be taken to ensure officers on the ground understand what is meant by a racist incident, such as a scheme in Lothian and Borders where officers use a credit-card-sized *aide-mémoire*.

It also proposes a national code of practice for reporting racist incidents and that the executive should consider setting up a 24-hour hotline for reporting such incidents, similar to the service available for victims of domestic abuse. A Scottish version of English police guidance on combating hate crime should also be produced.

Scottish justice minister Jim Wallace said: 'We have come a long way in the past two years and the steering group has made an invaluable contribution to this progress, providing outside scrutiny of the work of the police, crown office and others.

'But it is clear that much remains to be done. The handling of the murder of Surjit Singh Chhokar reminds us starkly of that. The actions

By David Mitchell

laid out in this review provide a challenging list of practical actions which the police, crown office, executive and others can address over the coming months and beyond.'

A Scottish version of English police guidance on combating hate crime should also be produced

Aamer Anwar, a leading race campaigner and spokesman for the Chhokar family justice campaign, which is calling for a public inquiry into the handling of the case of murdered Asian waiter Surjit Singh Chhokar, slammed the steering group as 'toothless' and accused the executive of watering down the recommendations of the Macpherson report.

'It's a superficial exercise going over the easiest parts without dealing with its fundamental aspects, which are about accountability and openness. They don't take account of the fact that officers on the beat have not taken on board the principles of Macpherson and the legacy of Stephen Lawrence,' he said.

'You won't find a single racist incident logged against a police officer in Scotland. Either they don't exist in Scotland or there is something wrong with the procedures and they haven't been changed. If racist officers are not sacked, this only increases the confidence of others who are racist.'

Mr Anwar said the measures themselves were welcome but failed to reach the heart of the problem. 'The Macpherson report was all about institutional racism – that people are denied access to the system and justice – and they haven't really tackled that. All those issues have been dodged,' he said.

Robina Qureshi, director of Positive Action in Housing, which targets racism and ethnic minority homelessness in Scotland, and a member of the steering group, is dismayed that the group has no teeth to back its recommendations.

'Efforts are being made, but not enough to say there is progress. We have no power to make anyone do anything. If they were clear and committed, we would have power behind what we are trying to do. Now, a year and a half later, it is just another report,' she said.

Ms Qureshi claimed the review didn't go far enough in tackling institutional racism. 'They are afraid to recognise that the problems are at the root of their own system. We would like a programme of radical change to directly address institutional racism. The best way of doing that is to have a multiracial task force in each department – police, judiciary, fiscal and crown office,' she said.

Vijay Patel, secretary of the black and ethnic minority infrastructure in Scotland, an umbrella group for black voluntary organisations, said the group's recommendations only scratched the surface of what was required.

'They are pretty weak and I suspect a number of people could have come up with them a year earlier without forming a committee. The nicest thing I can say is at least the executive and criminal justice system are actually speaking to people who understand the issues,' he said.

'Unless you understand the values involved, you are on a hiding to nothing. Across the executive, a number of civil servants are struggling with the notion because they don't understand the concept of discrimination. Only when you understand that, can you then think about how to deal with it personally and institutionally.'

© *Guardian Newspapers Limited 2001*

Britain: not the most racist country in Europe

The details of a new report into racism disprove the idea that the UK has the worst record for treating asylum seekers and refugees, writes the *Guardian*'s home affairs correspondent, Alan Travis

The idea that Britain is the most racist country in Europe when it comes to the treatment of asylum seekers and refugees is not only wide of the mark but also a gross misrepresentation of the report published today which has seemingly given further credence to the claim.

The Council of Europe's commission on racism and intolerance is right to highlight the persistent and acute problems in the treatment and media image of asylum seekers. This was especially true as its researchers based their findings on a visit in May 2000, immediately after the most virulent local election campaign that Britain had seen for nearly 20 years.

But it is completely wrong to claim that the report by the 43-nation human rights organisation in some way brands Britain as the 'most racist country in Europe'. In fact the commission published five separate reports yesterday on five different countries, including Austria, Macedonia and Albania.

The commission reserved its harshest words for Austria, where it says that existing anti-racism laws fail to protect black people, the use of racist propaganda in politics is widespread and the police attitudes are especially worrying.

Britain's record cannot possibly be compared with those of Macedonia and Albania, both of which have been the scene of violent campaigns against different minority ethnic groups, and which regularly lead to asylum seekers fleeing to the rest of Europe, including the UK.

The other country the commission looked at is Denmark, which is perhaps more comparable to Britain. But even in this country the Strasbourg researchers said that the prevailing political culture was of 'deep concern', probably even more so than Britain.

This week's report did not cover France and Germany but, by nearly every measure, Britain could not be said to be more racist than either country. Indeed, its most trenchant criticisms of the treatment of asylum seekers in Britain probably apply equally to Germany, as the British system is modelled on what happens in Germany.

The reasons for deep concern about the treatment of asylum seekers in Britain include fears about their detention and the powers of immigration officers. However, on a European scale Britain is by no means the worst country.

In fact, the Strasbourg report goes on to praise Britain for the progress it has made in the past two years in fighting institutional racism and placing a positive duty on public bodies to promote racial equality in the wake of the murder of black teenager, Stephen Lawrence.

Britain is not, despite what you may have heard, the most racist country in Europe.

© *Guardian Newspapers Limited 2001*

New safeguards for human rights

A new law, which came into force on 2 October, could provide invaluable new safeguards for immigrants, refugees, ethnic and racial minorities and asylum seekers in Britain. The Human Rights Act 1998 incorporates the European Convention on Human Rights (ECHR), which protects individuals' civil and political rights, into English law.

'The Act, which applies to public authorities and private organisations with public functions, has the potential to work in tandem with the new Race Relations (Amendment) Bill', said CRE chair Gurbux Singh. 'The new race law will outlaw discrimination in public functions not previously covered by the Race Relations Act and will introduce a new, enforceable, positive duty on public authorities to promote racial equality. Discrimination by public authorities will become twice as hard.'

The Human Rights Act sees the end of the age-old tradition that people can do whatever they please, unless they are specifically prohibited by law. For the first time people will have 'positive rights'. Although judges will not be able to overturn any laws made by parliament, they will be able to point out when laws are incompatible with the ECHR, and strike out secondary legislation – such as the regulations and orders issued by ministers.

The ECHR was drawn up by the Council of Europe after the Second World War and 41 countries are currently signed up to it. Incorporation of the ECHR into British law means that people will be able to take their cases directly to courts and tribunals in this country instead of going to the European Court of Human Rights in Strasbourg.

Public authorities – the judiciary, local, education and health authorities, and the police, prison and immigration services – will be called to account if their actions are incompatible with the ECHR. They will have to maintain a fair balance between the rights of individuals and the public interest.

The Human Rights Act does not provide blanket protection against discrimination, only against discrimination experienced in relation to the rights it guarantees. In certain specified circumstances those rights can be legitimately limited if the courts can show reasonable and objective justification. However, the Act has the welcome potential to redress serious injustices that people from ethnic minorities have endured. For example:

- families who are subjected to constant racist abuse from neighbours who are council tenants could take action under Article 8 and Protocol 1, Article 1, and, if the council fails to protect them, under Article 14 as well
- detention of, for example, Roma asylum seekers by the immigration service could be challenged under Article 5 and Article 8 together with Article 14

- a Muslim teacher in a state school who is dismissed for wearing a *hijaab* could challenge this under Article 9
- deaths in custody could be challenged under Article 2 and, given the disproportionate number of black men who have died in custody, under Article 14 as well
- school exclusions, which affect a disproportionate number of African Caribbean boys, could be challenged if there is evidence of discrimination (Protocol 1 Article 2 together with Article 14).

When the new Race Relations Act comes into force, certain types of conduct could be in breach of both the race and human rights legislation. For example:

- police forces using stop and search powers disproportionately against ethnic minorities, or immigration officers detaining people on the basis of racial stereotypes
- dress codes, which could be challenged under Article 10 as well as the new race law.

A handbook on how to use the HRA to challenge racism and racial discrimination will be produced by

the CRE, the Discrimination Law Association, the Immigration Law Practitioners' Association and the 1990 Trust in early 2000.

Human Rights Act 1998

Article 2 the right to life

Article 3 freedom from torture, inhuman or degrading treatment or punishment

Article 4 freedom from slavery and forced or compulsory labour

Article 5 freedom from arbitrary arrest or detention

Article 6 the right to fair trial and to be presumed innocent until proven guilty

Article 7 freedom from retrospective crime

Article 8 respect for private and family life

Article 9 freedom of thought, conscience and religion

Article 10 freedom of expression

Article 11 freedom of assembly and association

Article 12 the right to marry and have a family

Protocol 1, Article 1 the right to peaceful enjoyment of property

Protocol 1, Article 2 the right to education

Protocol 1, Article 3 the right to free and fair elections

Article 14 the enjoyment of all these rights without discrimination on any ground

- The above information is an extract from *Connections*, the quarterly magazine produced by the Commission for Racial Equality (CRE). See page 41 for address details.

© Commission for Racial Equality (CRE)

Protecting children from racism and racial abuse

A research review. Summary of research and findings.

The impact of racism

- Racism has been defined in many ways, but a consensus has emerged that issues of power and domination are as important as those of prejudice.
- Research has consistently demonstrated that children from ethnic minorities suffer many forms of disadvantage in British society, and that this can include poorer health, poverty and educational under-achievement. Effects are not necessarily uniform, with minorities being differentially affected and some variation by gender.

Research on racial abuse of children

- There is only a limited amount of research specifically relating to the issue of racial abuse of children but two discrete bodies of research provide insights into this aspect of children's lives; racial bullying within school settings and racial violence within the community. Although these areas do not compre-

By Christine Barter

hensively address the issue, they provide valuable messages for agencies working with minority ethnic children and families.

- Children from ethnic minorities are more likely to experience bullying than their white counterparts.
- The most common expression of racism is through racist name-calling, which is often viewed by adults as trivial, although its impact on children can be profound.
- Although research evidence is limited, what is available does imply that racial bullying frequently involves the use of violence.
- In areas where there are few children from minority ethnic communities these children may be particularly vulnerable to racial abuse. The effect is heightened by the lack of access to support from other minority ethnic children.

- Children's racism should not be viewed as consistent or unified. Their participation in racism is complex and often contradictory. Many children hold anti-racist beliefs and condemn discrimination whilst also perpetrating racist behaviour.

Violent racism

- A small body of research has emerged which addresses adolescents' experiences and perceptions of violent racism, both as victims and perpetrators. These have usually occurred in 'problem' areas where high levels of racial violence were previously identified.
- One of the consequences of focusing on 'extreme' areas is that much of the research has been undertaken in working-class localities. The prevalence and impact of racial abuse in predominately middle-class areas has yet to be addressed.
- Many victims of racial violence are adolescents, although younger children can also suffer.

- Perpetrators of racial violence are mostly either adolescents or young adults.
- Violence against ethnic minority groups is persistent, patterned, and long-term in the way that it affects individuals and the places where they live.
- In areas with high levels of racial abuse and harassment, violent racism is often seen by white people as a routine aspect of daily life rather than as a deviant or pathological activity.

Disability and racial abuse

- Although evidence is scarce, studies do suggest that disabled minority ethnic children and adults commonly experience both verbal and physical forms of racial abuse and harassment. It is unclear how the dual dimension of disability and race makes their experiences different to those of non-disabled children.

Racial abuse in the family

- Some children of mixed parentage can experience racial abuse, both verbal and physical, within their family settings, most commonly by a white parent or relative, although occasionally by the ethnic minority family members.

Responding to racial abuse of children

The evidence reviewed demonstrated the five main factors that strategies to challenge racial abuse and harassment need to address:

Local cultures of racism

- The manner in which racism is constructed, understood and mediated in different localities determines the extent of racial abuse and harassment in the area and its particular nature and dynamic. Frequently, the views held by perpetrators of racial harassment and violence towards ethnic minorities are shared by the wider communities to which they belong. Perpetrators view this as legitimising their actions. Consequently any strategies to combat racial abuse must also address racism in its wider context.

Wider impact of racial violence

- Any discussion on the impact of violence on ethnic minority communities must acknowledge that the fear and anxiety extend far beyond the individual victim and affect the whole community.
- Racist motivation can transform even apparently trivial incidents into something much more disturbing and frightening both for victims and other members of the ethnic group.
- Children do not necessarily have to be direct victims to suffer the effects of racial abuse. The targeting of their relatives or communities as a whole will inevitably impact on their lives.

White people as victims of racial abuse

- In many victim accounts there are reports of attacks on white as well as ethnic minority victims.
- The intensity and nature of the violence is very different for the two groups, with ethnic minority children much more likely to experience repeat victimisation. One study found that white victimisation was the result of ethnic minorities' resistance to racial abuse linked to territorial dominance. How prevalent are attacks on white children in other circumstances or on children and young people from white ethnic minority groups such as Jewish or Irish populations is unknown.

Reproduction of racism

- Little is known about how racist views are reproduced in children. Existing research is ambiguous. Some shows that racism is passed generationally through families and that children are racist because their parents have taught them to be. Other research has found that many children have very distinct views from their parents concerning race and that they themselves establish the culture of racism.
- Wider societal and institutional forms of racism perpetuate racist beliefs and ideologies in the population and make it easier for people to commit racist acts.

Backlash against anti-racist policies

- Responses against racism and racial abuse that are not presented in an appropriate form may create an 'anti-racist backlash', by being perceived as 'unfair' by the target community. Insensitive anti-racist strategies may inadvertently give strength to racist beliefs rather than challenge racism. Strategies to combat racist violence also need to incorporate an understanding of how perpetrators see the world.

Challenging racism

- Although the family structure is an important site of resistance to racism, research highlights that many minority ethnic children do not discuss their experiences of racial abuse with parents or other family members.
- Ethnic minority young people are not passive recipients of racism – they employ a range of strategies when confronted with racial abuse.
- It is important to produce integrated strategies, involving a number of agencies, to combat racist abuse both in the school setting and in the local community.
- To date, the majority of responses have focused on the victims of racial harassment, but the effectiveness of these programmes is debatable. Agencies also need to undertake both preventive and interventive programmes focusing on perpetrators.
- There is a need for approaches which are based on children's actual experiences and perceptions rather than adult constructions of the problem.

Social services response to racial abuse

- Official child care procedures and guidance emphasise cultural sensitivity rather than requiring agencies to adopt pro-active approaches to challenging racism.
- The review found no research-based literature pertaining to the role of the child protection system in responding to the racial abuse of children. Social work texts assert that although racial abuse does constitute child abuse it should not generally be addressed through the formal child protection system as its causes and manifestations are different from abuse within families. The exception to this is intra-familial racial abuse which is a form of emotional abuse.

Conclusions and recommendations

- Research on health, education, employment and identity shows differences between minority ethnic communities. Research on children and racism similarly needs to address differences between communities, alongside the impact of age, gender and disability.
- There is a need for research in four main areas in order to inform child welfare responses to racial abuse:

Perpetrator studies

Studies need to identify what factors motivate and support young children, adolescents and adults to commit acts of racial abuse, and what are the most effective ways of combating these.

Children's perceptions of racial abuse

We need a better understanding of children's perceptions and experiences of racial abuse, its impact on their lives, and what forms of assistance they perceive as being the most helpful and appropriate.

Resilience to racial abuse

Research on resistance to racial abuse needs to be developed, especially studies exploring factors associated with resilient children, families and local communities.

Child protection

Research needs to be done on the interface between child protection and racial abuse, in particular the impact of the child protection system on children from different communities and on racial abuse in the context of other forms of child abuse.

- The full report *Protecting Children from Racism and Racial Abuse* ISBN: 0 902498 82 7 is priced at £17.25 and available from the NSPCC. See page 41 for address details.

© NSPCC 2000

UK whites will be minority by 2100

By Anthony Browne

Whites will be an ethnic minority in Britain by the end of the century. Analysis of official figures indicate that, at current fertility rates and levels of immigration, there will be more non-whites than whites by 2100.

It would be the first time in history that a major indigenous population has voluntarily become a minority, rather than through war, famine or disease. Whites will be a minority in London by 2010.

In the early 1950s there were only a few tens of thousands of non-whites in the UK. By 1991 that had risen to 3 million – 6 per cent of the population. The population of ethnic minorities has been growing at between 2 and 4 per cent a year. Net immigration has been running at record levels, with 185,000 newcomers last year.

Government forecasts suggest that immigration on its own will be responsible for half the growth of the British population over the next couple of decades.

New immigrants, who are on average younger than the population at large, also tend to have higher fertility rates. In contrast, the population of white British citizens is static. Their fertility rate is very low – at under 2 children per woman – and there is overall emigration of British citizens.

The analysis of the figures showed that if the population of ethnic minorities grows at 4 per cent a year, whites will become a minority before 2100. The demographer who made the calculation wished to remain anonymous for fear of accusations of racism.

© *Guardian Newspapers Limited 2000*

ADDITIONAL RESOURCES

You might like to contact the following organisations for further information. Due to the increasing cost of postage, many organisations cannot respond to enquiries unless they receive a stamped, addressed envelope.

Black Information Link
The 1990 Trust
9 Cranmer Road
London, SW9 6EJ
Tel: 020 7582 1990
Fax: 020 7717 1585
E-mail: blink1990@gn.apc.org
Web site: www.blink.org.uk
Black Information Link is run by the 1990 Trust, a national Black organisation.

British Humanist Association
47 Theobald's Road
London, WC1X 8SP
Tel: 020 7430 0908
Fax: 020 7430 1271
E-mail: info@humanism.org.uk
Web site: www.humanism.org.uk
Publishes a wide range of free briefings including the issues of racism and discrimination and prejudice.

ChildLine
2nd Floor Royal Mail Building
50 Studd Street
London, N1 0QW
Tel: 020 7239 1000
Fax: 020 7239 1001
E-mail: reception@childline.org.uk
Web site: www.childline.org.uk
ChildLine provides a confidential phone counselling service for any child with any problem 24 hours a day. Children or young people can phone or write free of charge about problems of any kind to: ChildLine, Freepost 1111, London N1 0BR, Tel: Freephone 0800 1111.

Commission for Racial Equality (CRE)
Elliot House, 10-12 Allington Street
London, SW1E 5EH
Tel: 020 7828 7022
Fax: 020 7931 0429
E-mail: info@cre.gov.uk
Web site: www.cre.gov.uk
The CRE is working for racial equality for a just society, which gives everyone an equal chance to work, learn and live free from discrimination and prejudice. Ask for their publications list.

Exposure Magazine
The Bigger Shoe Box
Muswell Hill Centre
Hillfield Park
London, N10 3QJ
Tel: 020 8883 0260
Fax: 020 8883 2906
E-mail: editor@exposure.org.uk
Web site: www.exposure.org.uk
Exposure's vision is to be a leading youth media organisation, helping young people in Haringey, in London and beyond to achieve their full potential in media work, extending from magazine production into design services, internet services, video and audio production.

The Industrial Society
49 Calthorpe Road
Birmingham, B15 1TH
Tel: 01870 400 1000
Fax: 01780 400 1099
E-mail: customercentre@indsoc.co.uk
Web site: www.indsoc.co.uk
The Industrial Society is an independent, not-for-profit campaigning body with over 10,000 member organisations from every part of the economy.

Joseph Rowntree Foundation (JRF)
The Homestead, 40 Water End
York, YO30 6WP
Tel: 01904 629241
Fax: 01904 620072
E-mail: infor@jrf.org.uk
Web site: www.jrf.org.uk
JRF is an independent, non-political body which funds programmes of research and innovative development in the fields of housing, social care and social policy.

Kick it Out
c/o Business Design Centre
52 Upper Street
London, N1 0QH
Tel: 020 7288 6012
Fax: 020 7288 6042
E-mail: kick-racism@kick-it-out.demon.co.uk
Web site: www.kickitout.org

Kick It Out was established as an independent organisation and took up the role of furthering the objectives of highlighting and campaigning against racism in football at all levels.

NSPCC – National Society for the Prevention of Cruelty to Children
National Centre, 42 Curtain Road
London, EC2A 3NH
Tel: 020 7825 2500
Fax: 020 7825 2525
E-mail: info@nspcc.org.uk
Web site: www.nspcc.org.uk
The National Society for the Prevention of Cruelty to Children (NSPCC) is the UK's leading charity specialising in child protection and the prevention of cruelty to children.

Show Racism the Red Card
PO Box 141
Whitley Bay
Tyne And Wear, NE26 3RG
Tel: 0191 291 0160
Fax: 0191 291 0160
E-mail: info@theredcard.org
Web site: www.srtrc.org
Show Racism the Red Card is sponsored by the Professional Footballers' Association, the public sector trade union, Unison, and the European Commission.

Trades Union Congress – Equal Rights Department (TUC)
Congress House
23-28 Great Russell Street
London, WC1B 3LS
Tel: 020 7636 4030
Fax: 020 7636 0632
E-mail: info@tuc.org.uk
Web site: www.tuc.org.uk
The TUC has over 75 member trade unions, representing nearly seven million people from all walks of life. They are Britain's largest voluntary organisation. They campaign on concerns in the world of work and build links with all political parties, business and the community.

INDEX

Independence Web News

Back | Forward | Home | Reload | Images | Open | Print | Find | Stop

Live Home Page | Search | Computer | Support | System

* * * * *

The Internet has been likened to shopping in a supermarket without aisles. The press of a button on a Web browser can bring up thousands of sites but working your way through them to find what you want can involve long and frustrating on-line searches.

And unfortunately many sites contain inaccurate, misleading or heavily biased information. Our researchers have therefore undertaken an extensive analysis to bring you a selection of quality Web site addresses.

Black Information Link
www.blink.org.uk
Black Information Link is run by the 1990 Trust, a national Black organisation. The site includes sections on everything from art and culture, to the Stephen Lawrence campaign, and human rights.

British Humanist Association
www.humanism.org.uk
Go to Ethical Issues for a full list of topics shown on their web site.

Commission for Racial Equality (CRE)
www.cre.gov.uk
Click on any item in the list of contents at the top left of the home page to go straight to a more detailed list of the topics you can reach under that heading. A wide range of CRE factsheets can be downloaded as PDF files.

Joseph Rowntree Foundation (JRF)
www.jrf.org.uk
This web site contains several hundred research summaries (*Findings*) which can be accessed by key word. Press releases and publications can also be accessed by clicking on the relevant icon in the navigation panel.

Show Racism the Red Card
www.srtrc.org
This web site has a lot of resources which schools can order: videos, CD ROMS and free posters as well as their free magazine.

Trades Union Congress – Equal Rights Department (TUC)
www.tuc.org.uk
Click on Equality and look under Black Workers. Here you can find recent TUC material on racial equality.

ACKNOWLEDGEMENTS

The publisher is grateful for permission to reproduce the following material.

While every care has been taken to trace and acknowledge copyright, the publisher tenders its apology for any accidental infringement or where copyright has proved untraceable. The publisher would be pleased to come to a suitable arrangement in any such case with the rightful owner.

Chapter One: Racism in the Community

Discrimination and prejudice, © British Humanist Association, *Racism today*, © Show Racism the Red Card, *The rise of the Little Englanders*, © Guardian Newspapers Limited 2000, *A black and white issue*, © Exposure Magazine, *Nazi piece of work*, © Exposure Magazine, *Race crime*, © Guardian Newspapers Limited 2001, *Racial crime vs. ethnic population*, © Crown copyright is reproduced with the permission of the Controller of Her Majesty's Stationery Office, *Race and the criminal justice system*, © Crown copyright is reproduced with the permission of the Controller of Her Majesty's Stationery Office, *Police 'show no race bias in searches'*, © Telegraph Group Limited, London 2000, *Asylum seekers*, © The 1990 Trust, *Ethnic minorities grow to 1 in 10*, © Guardian Newspapers Limited 2001, *Race and the workplace*, © Guardian Newspapers Limited 2000, *Harassment at work*, © Race Relations Employment Advisory Service (RREAS), *Exposing racism at work*, © Trades Union Congress (TUC), *Racist firms keep black unemployment high*, © Guardian Newspapers Limited 2001, *Employment*, © Crown copyright is reproduced with the permission of the Controller of Her Majesty's Stationery Office, *Racial discrimination*, © The Industrial Society, *Racism and xenophobia in English football*, © Kick It Out, *'There's no racism in football . . .'*, Kick It Out, *The misguided campaign for Asians to play football*, © Guardian Newspapers Limited 2001.

Chapter Two: Tackling Racism

Let's beat racism, © ChildLine, *Action being taken to tackle racial harassment*, © Joseph Rowntree Foundation, *Racist bullying*, © Show Racism the Red Card, *Teaching tolerance in the classroom*, © Commission for Racial Equality (CRE), *Black culture 'holding back' boys*, © Telegraph Group Limited, London 2000, *Britain: a racist society?*, © Market & Opinion Research International (MORI), *Embracing the need to build an inclusive society*, © Guardian Newspapers Limited 2000, *Public sector forced to tackle racism*, © Guardian Newspapers Limited 2001, *Satisfaction with the Police*, © Market & Opinion Research International (MORI), *Scots under fire*, © Guardian Newspapers Limited 2001, *Britain: not the most racist country in Europe*, © Guardian Newspapers Limited 2001, *New safeguards for human rights*, © Commission for Racial Equality (CRE), *Protecting children from racism and racial abuse*, © NSPCC, *UK whites will be minority by 2100*, © Guardian Newspapers Limited 2000.

Photographs and illustrations:

Pages 1, 5, 10, 23, 27, 33: Pumpkin House, pages 3, 9, 12, 15, 20, 24, 29, 35, 37, 39: Simon Kneebone

Craig Donnellan
Cambridge
April, 2001